Breathing Well

By Paul Bennett

Silver Press
Parsippany, New Jersey

First published in the U.K. in 1997 by
Belitha Press Limited
London House, Great Eastern Wharf
Parkgate Road, London SW11 4NQ

Editor: Veronica Ross
Series designer: Hayley Cove
Photographer: Claire Paxton
Illustrator: Cilla Eurich
Picture researcher: Diana Morris
Consultants: Jo Ormisher/Elizabeth Atkinson

Published in the United States in 1998 by
Silver Press
A Division of Simon & Schuster
299 Jefferson Road
Parsippany, New Jersey 07054-0480

Library of Congress Cataloging-in-Publication Data
Bennett, Paul, 1954–
Breathing well/by Paul Bennett.
Originally published: London: Belitha Press, 1997.
Includes index.
Summary: Explains how and why we breathe; the functions of
chest, lungs, blood, and heart in this process; problems related to
breathing, and what to do when we cough or sneeze
1. Respiration—Juvenile literature. [1. Respiration.] I. Title.
II. Series: Bodyworks (Parsippany, N.J.)
QP121.B37   1998   96–53555
612.2—dc21   CIP   AC
ISBN 0-382-39777-0 (LSB)   1 2 3 4 5 6 7 8 9 10
ISBN 0-382-39778-9 (pbk)   1 2 3 4 5 6 7 8 9 10

Printed in Hong Kong

Photo credits
Bubbles: 9t Ian West. NASA: 22. Science Photo Library:
13t Alfred Pasiekia; 15c CNRI; 25t Eye of Science. Still
Pictures: 24 Thomas Raupach. Zefa: 23b.

Thanks to models Topel, Jodie, Ricky, Bianca, Meera.

Words in **bold** are explained in the list of useful words
on pages 30 and 31.

Contents

Why do I need to breathe?

You need to breathe to stay alive.

You breathe all the time without thinking about it.

You breathe when you are asleep and when you brush your teeth.

4

When you breathe, air is sucked into your **lungs**. A **gas** called oxygen is in the air. Without oxygen you would die.

The oxygen is used by your body to make **energy**. You need energy when you play sports, read a book, or paint a picture, and for everything else you do.

Breathing in

You breathe in through your nose or mouth. Air goes down your throat in a tube called your windpipe.

Inside your chest the windpipe splits into two tubes, which take the air into your lungs.

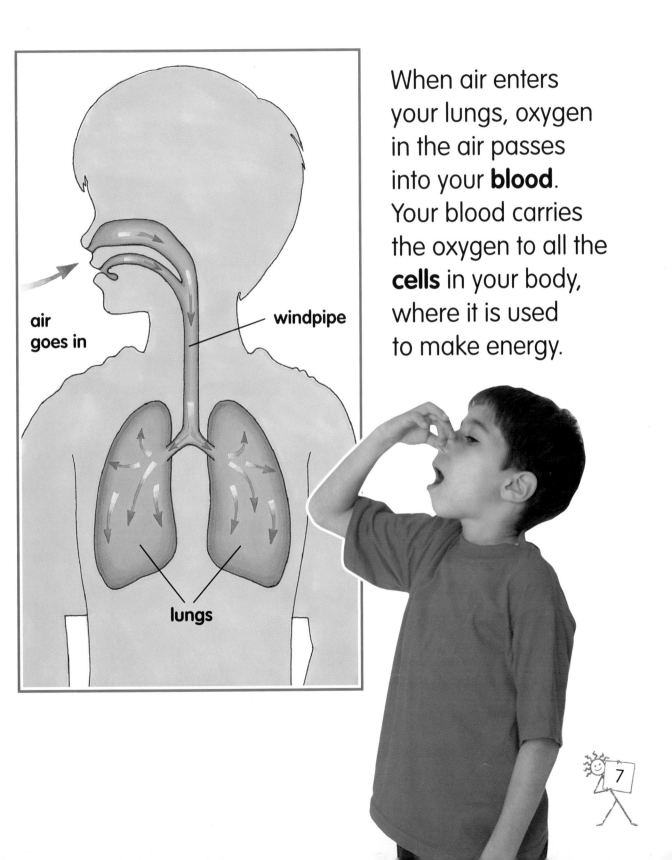

air goes in

windpipe

lungs

When air enters your lungs, oxygen in the air passes into your **blood**. Your blood carries the oxygen to all the **cells** in your body, where it is used to make energy.

Breathing out

When you breathe out, used air is squeezed out of your lungs, up your windpipe, and out of your nose or mouth.

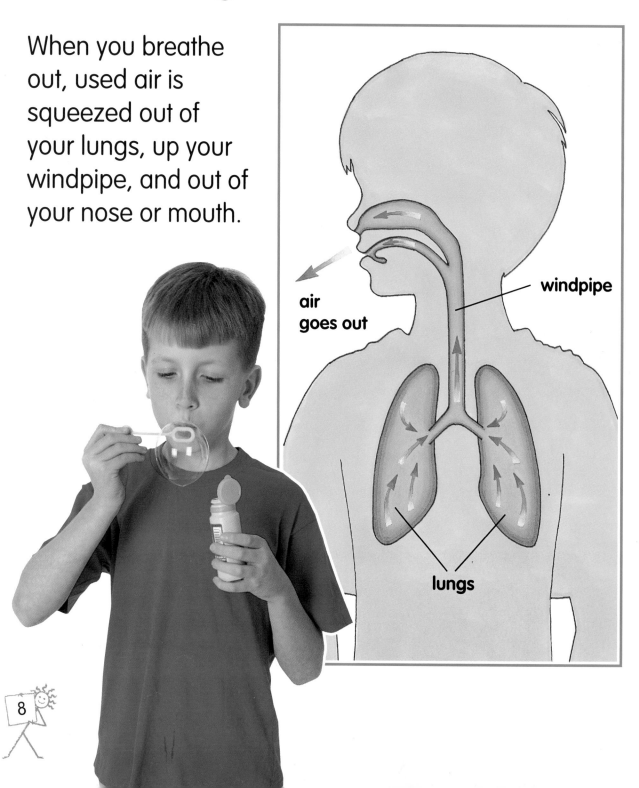

air goes out

windpipe

lungs

8

The air you breathe out has water in it. Breathe out deeply on a cold day. Can you see the water droplets?

A gas called carbon dioxide is in used air, too. The water and carbon dioxide leave your body when you breathe out.

You can blow out about two quarts of air in one try. That's enough to fill a balloon.

9

Your chest

Your lungs are inside your chest. They are protected by the **bones** that make up your **rib cage**.

Stand in front of a mirror and take a deep breath. Your chest becomes bigger.

At the same time, your **diaphragm** moves down. There is now more space for your lungs to **expand**, and air rushes in to fill them.

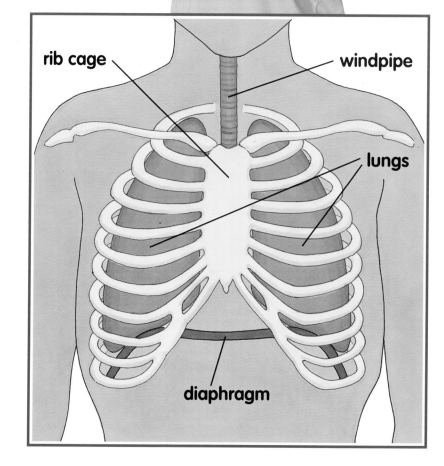

rib cage

windpipe

lungs

diaphragm

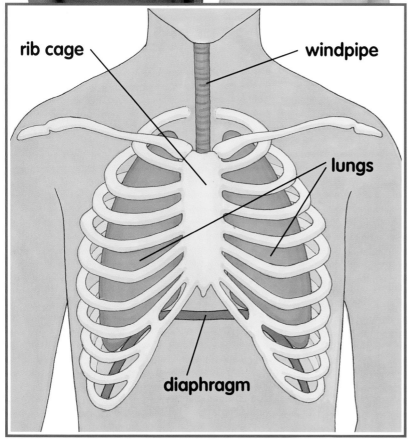

When you breathe out, your chest becomes smaller, and your diaphragm relaxes and moves up.

rib cage

windpipe

lungs

diaphragm

There is now less space inside your chest. Used air is squeezed up and out of your body.

Inside your lungs

Your lungs are like large sponges, but they hold air, not water.

Inside your lungs the air passes into lots of tiny tubes, which take the oxygen into your **bloodstream**.

The air tubes
in your lungs
split into
smaller
and smaller
tubes, like
the branches
on a tree.

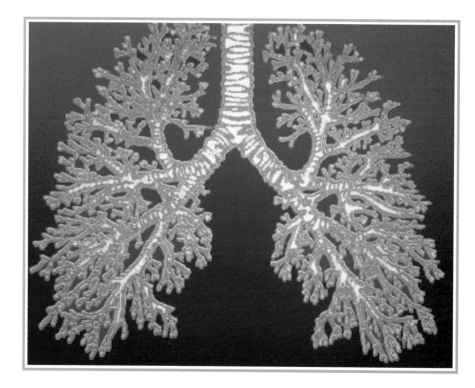

The smallest tubes end in
tiny air sacs, like the ones
shown here. The air sacs
are covered in very tiny
tubes called capillaries.

Oxygen from the air sacs
passes through your
capillaries and goes
into your blood.

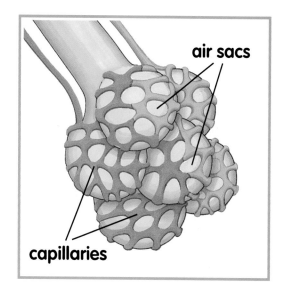

air sacs

capillaries

Your blood

Blood is a liquid that carries oxygen from your lungs all around your body. The oxygen is carried in millions of cells called red blood cells.

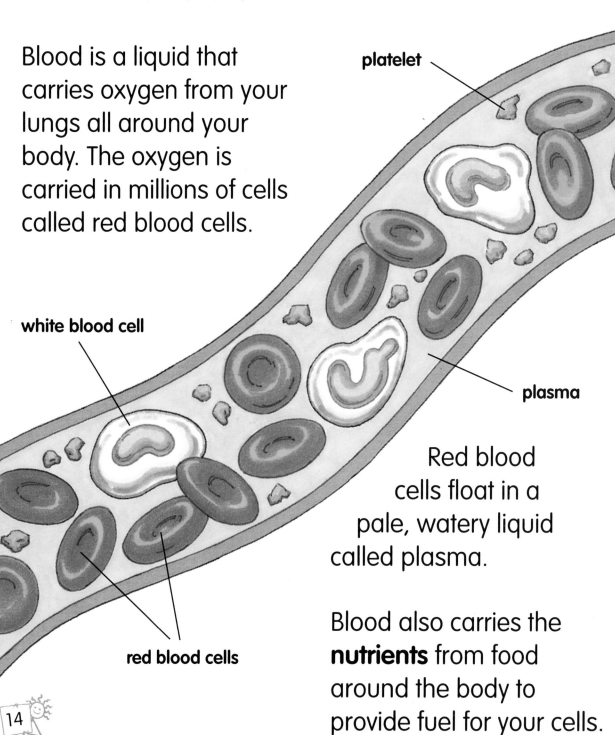

platelet

white blood cell

plasma

red blood cells

Red blood cells float in a pale, watery liquid called plasma.

Blood also carries the **nutrients** from food around the body to provide fuel for your cells.

There are other cells in your blood. White blood cells, like the one shown here, attack germs that enter your body.

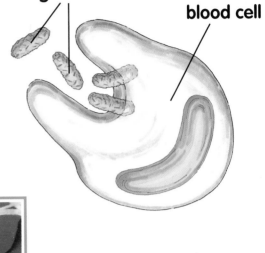

germs

white blood cell

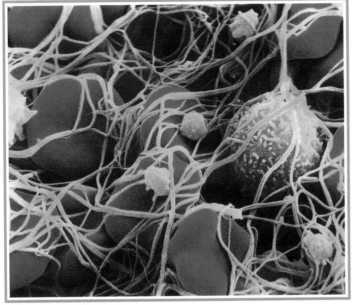

This is a photograph of a blood **clot**, taken through a **microscope**. Cells called platelets help your blood to clot and form a **scab** when you cut yourself.

A seven-year-old contains about three quarts of blood.

15

What is my heart like?

Your heart is a **muscle** about the size of your fist. It works like a powerful pump, sending blood to all parts of your body.

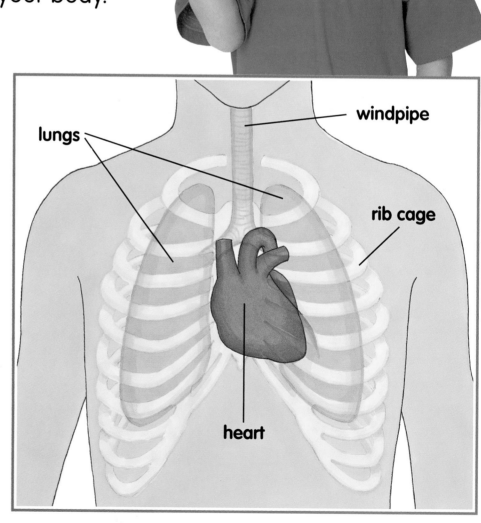

lungs

windpipe

rib cage

heart

Your heart never stops beating. Every time it beats, it pumps blood around your body.

You can feel your heart beating when you exercise.

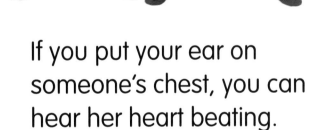

If you put your ear on someone's chest, you can hear her heart beating.

A seven-year-old child's heart beats about 80–100 times a minute.

Your veins and arteries

Blood is pumped from your heart and carried around your body in tubes called blood vessels.

The blood vessels that carry blood away from your heart are called arteries.

Each artery branches into smaller and smaller tubes. They lead into a network of capillaries.

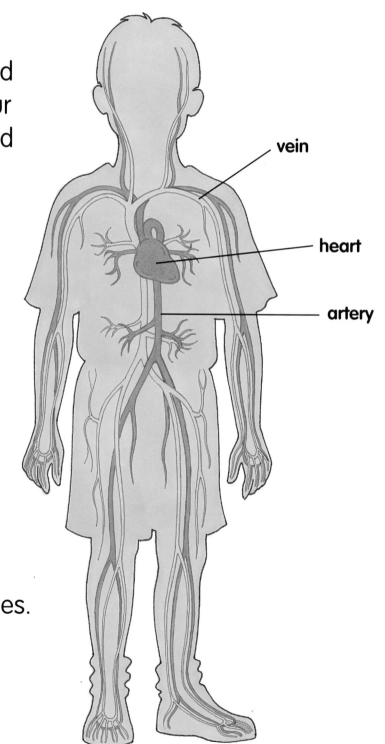

vein

heart

artery

Veins carry the blood
back to your heart,
which pumps it to
your lungs
and back.

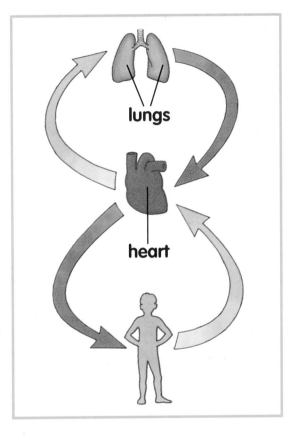

lungs

heart

In this way blood
flows around and
around your body.
This is called
circulation.

You can see your
veins on the back
of your hands.

Out of breath

When you are sitting still, you need to breathe only about 20 times a minute. Count the number of times you breathe in and out in a minute.

When you are resting, you do not need so much energy, so you breathe more slowly and your heart beats more slowly.

Try exercising hard for a few minutes. How many times a minute do you breathe now?

You need to take in lots more air when you exercise, so you breathe faster.

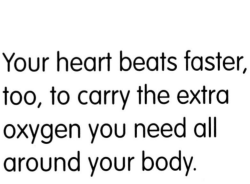

Your heart beats faster, too, to carry the extra oxygen you need all around your body.

The air around you

Air is all around you. It is made up mainly of two gases, oxygen and nitrogen.

The higher up you go, the less oxygen there is in the air.

If you traveled high up into the sky in a hot-air balloon, you would need a supply of oxygen to help you to breathe normally.

There is no air in space, so astronauts must wear a special suit that has its own air supply.

You cannot breathe under water, so you must hold your breath.

Divers wear air tanks to help them breathe under water.

Breathing problems

The air around us is made dirty by smoke from factories, cars, and trucks. **Polluted air** can damage your lungs and cause breathing problems.

People who smoke often have a bad cough and find it difficult to breathe. Lung and heart diseases can be caused by smoking.

Pollen and dust mites can also cause breathing problems. This is a picture of a dust mite seen under a microscope.

A common breathing problem is asthma. People with asthma can use an inhaler. This puffs out a special medicine that helps to keep the tubes in the lungs open.

Mouths and noses

Your nose is full of hairs that trap any dust or dirt that goes up your nose. Any tiny specks that reach your air tubes are gently swept away from your lungs by tiny hairs.

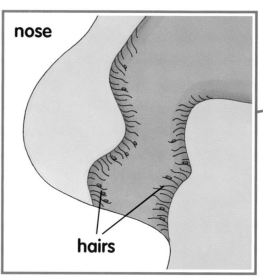

nose

hairs

A sneeze or cough clears your nose or throat and blows dust and pollen out.

26

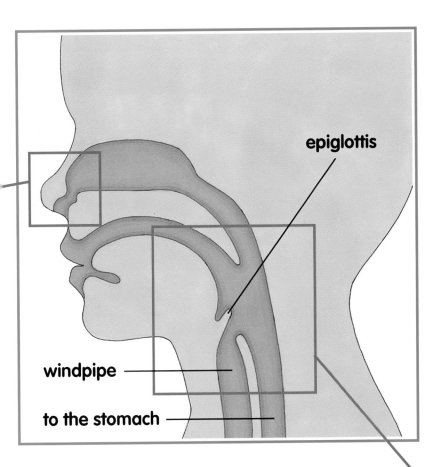

epiglottis

windpipe

to the stomach

If you are in a hurry and swallow food too fast, it may go down the wrong way. When this happens, a cough blows the food out.

The tube that your food goes down is behind your windpipe. When you swallow, a flap called the epiglottis closes over the entrance to the windpipe.

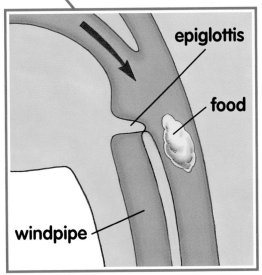

epiglottis

food

windpipe

Making sounds

The air you breathe out is used for talking. Air travels up your windpipe and through your **voice box** to make sounds.

Sounds are made into words by your mouth. Look in a mirror and see how you use your lips, tongue, teeth, and cheeks to make words.

Hiccups are caused when your diaphragm suddenly tightens and you take in short, sudden gasps of air.

When you laugh, you let out air in a quick series of short breaths. You sigh with a long breath out and yawn with a deep breath in.

Useful words

Blood
The red liquid that is pumped around your body by your heart.

Bloodstream
The flow of blood around your body.

Bones
The strong and hard parts inside your body.

Cells
Tiny parts that make up your body.

Clot
A thick lump of blood.

Diaphragm
A thin sheet of muscles and tendons under the lungs that tightens and relaxes as you breathe in and out.

Energy
What you need to be able to play and work without feeling tired.

Expand
To become larger.

Gas
Something that is like air, not solid and not liquid. Oxygen and nitrogen are two of the gases that make up air.

Lungs
The spongy areas in your chest that you use when breathing.

Microscope
An instrument that you use to look at things closely. It makes small things look bigger.

Muscle

A soft, stretchy part inside your body that makes you move. In your heart the muscle draws together and stretches out, causing your heart to beat.

Nutrients

The useful parts of food that your body needs to stay healthy.

Pollen

A fine dust found in flowers.

Polluted air

Air that is made dirty by the dangerous gases pumped out by factories and motor vehicles. It can damage people's lungs.

Rib cage

The bones in your chest that protect your heart and lungs.

Scab

The hard crust that forms over a cut or scratch.

Voice box

The part of your windpipe that makes sounds so that you can talk.

Index

PEDIATRIC NURSE PRACTITIONER CERTIFICATION

Study Question Book

Third Edition

Edited by

JoAnne Silbert-Flagg, DNP, CPNP, IBCLC

Assistant Professor
Johns Hopkins University School of Nursing
Baltimore, Maryland

Elizabeth Sloand, PhD, CRNP

Assistant Professor
Coordinator, Pediatric Nurse Practitioner Track
Johns Hopkins University School of Nursing
Baltimore, Maryland

JONES & BARTLETT
LEARNING

World Headquarters

Jones & Bartlett Learning
40 Tall Pine Drive
Sudbury, MA 01776
978-443-5000
info@jblearning.com
www.jblearning.com

Jones & Bartlett Learning
Canada
6339 Ormindale Way
Mississauga, Ontario L5V 1J2
Canada

Jones & Bartlett Learning
International
Barb House, Barb Mews
London W6 7PA
United Kingdom

Jones & Bartlett Learning books and products are available through most bookstores and online booksellers. To contact Jones & Bartlett Learning directly, call 800-832-0034, fax 978-443-8000, or visit our website, www.jblearning.com.

Substantial discounts on bulk quantities of Jones & Bartlett Learning publications are available to corporations, professional associations, and other qualified organizations. For details and specific discount information, contact the special sales department at Jones & Bartlett Learning via the above contact information or send an email to specialsales@jblearning.com.

The authors, editor, and publisher have made every effort to provide accurate information. However, they are not responsible for errors, omissions, or for any outcomes related to the use of the contents of this book and take no responsibility for the use of the products and procedures described. Treatments and side effects described in this book may not be applicable to all people; likewise, some people may require a dose or experience a side effect that is not described herein. Drugs and medical devices are discussed that may have limited availability controlled by the Food and Drug Administration (FDA) for use only in a research study or clinical trial. Research, clinical practice, and government regulations often change the accepted standard in this field. When consideration is being given to use of any drug in the clinical setting, the health care provider or reader is responsible for determining FDA status of the drug, reading the package insert, and reviewing prescribing information for the most up-to-date recommendations on dose, precautions, and contraindications, and determining the appropriate usage for the product. This is especially important in the case of drugs that are new or seldom used.

Production Credits
Publisher: Kevin Sullivan
Acquisitions Editor: Amy Sibley
Associate Editor: Patricia Donnelly
Editorial Assistant: Rachel Shuster
Production Editor: Amanda Clerkin
Marketing Manager: Rebecca Wasley
V.P., Manufacturing and Inventory Control: Therese Connell
Composition: DSCS/Absolute Service, Inc.
Cover Design: Kristin E. Parker
Cover Image: © Hocusfocus/Dreamstime.com
Printing and Binding: Malloy, Inc.
Cover Printing: Malloy, Inc.

6048

Printed in the United States of America
14 13 12 11 10   10 9 8 7 6 5 4 3 2 1

Contents

Preface

Jones & Bartlett Learning is pleased to introduce the third edition of the *Pediatric Nurse Practitioner Certification Study Question Book*. This book will help the user to be successful in the examination process. These questions differ from those that are included in the *Pediatric Nurse Practitioner Certification Review Guide*, thus giving the reader an additional set of practice questions. This book has been developed to enhance your test-taking skills according to the principles of test taking found in the chapter titled Test-Taking Strategies and Skills in the *Pediatric Nurse Practitioner Certification Review Guide*. This book should not be the only source used to prepare for the pediatric or family nurse practitioner certification examination. Instead, it should be used in conjunction with the *Pediatric Nurse Practitioner Certification Review Guide*, a review course, and home study program to provide a comprehensive approach to successful preparation for the examination.

Taking practice test questions is an important exercise in the certification examination preparation process, but only one strategy to be used in combination with a strong knowledge base. Success in the certification examination area depends upon excellent test-taking skills and a comprehensive understanding of the materials covered by the examination. As a nurse practitioner seeking certification, you must not lose sight of the purpose of certification: a mastery of essential materials for competent and superior practice.

Certification boards provide directives and materials for study. They also supply content outlines and sample test questions to examinees prior to the examinations. Individual testing boards also provide specific areas of study, including suggested readings for each examination.

Board certified nurse practitioners have prepared and reviewed this question book. There are over 300 problem-oriented board-type multiple choice questions that are divided according to content area, with answers and rationales. Every effort has been made to develop sample questions that are representative of the types of questions that may be found on the certification examination; however, style and format of the examination may differ. Practicing tests, understanding test-taking strategies, and, above all, knowing your subject will lead to success.

Authors' Note

This question book is designed in a multiple choice, self-testing, question and answer format. Answers are provided with rationales. The *Study Question Book* is a great companion to the *Certification Review Guide*. The editors wish much success to the users of this guide in their future careers as advanced practice nurses.

I want to take the opportunity to thank Beth (Elizabeth Sloand) for her dedication and expertise as coeditor for the *Pediatric Nurse Practitioner Certification Study Question Book* and the companion *Pediatric Nurse Practitioner Certification Review Guide*. As the readers of these books advance in their profession, they will find their colleagues to be their most valued asset. I would like to thank Anne Belcher and Mary Terhaar, both faculty members at Johns Hopkins University School of Nursing, for their most appreciated assistance in the development of my career.

JoAnne Silbert-Flagg

Contributors

Peggy Dorr, MS, CRNP
Pediatric Nurse Practitioner
Division of Pediatric Cardiology
University of Maryland Medical Center
Baltimore, Maryland

Malinda D. Duke, CPNP, CDE
Pediatric Endocrinology
Joslin Diabetes Center
University of Maryland
Baltimore, Maryland

Marlo A. Eldridge, MSN, CPNP
Co-Director
Voiding Improvement Program of the Brady
    Urological Institute
Johns Hopkins Hospital
Baltimore, Maryland

Jeanne Steman Findlay, CRNP, CCRP
Instructor
Department of Dermatology
Johns Hopkins University
School of Medicine
Baltimore, Maryland

Rita Marie John, EdD, DNP, CPNP
Pediatric Nurse Practitioner/Neonatal Nurse
Practitioner Program Director
Columbia University
School of Nursing
New York, New York

Rachel Lyons, DNP, CPNP-AC/PC
Assistant Professor of Clinical Nursing
Pediatric Orthopaedic Surgery
Morgan Stanley Children's Hospital
    of New York Presbyterian
Columbia University
School of Nursing
New York, New York

Maureen C. Maguire, MSN, RN, PNP
Assistant Professor
Johns Hopkins University
School of Nursing
Baltimore, Maryland

Jody K. Roblyer, MS, CRNP-P
Clinical Instructor
Johns Hopkins University
School of Nursing
Baltimore, Maryland

MaryLou C. Rosenblatt, RN, MS, CPNP
Lead Nurse Practitioner, Adolescent
    Medicine Clinic
Faculty LEAH (Leadership Education in
    Adolescent Health)
Johns Hopkins Hospital
Baltimore, Maryland

Janet S. Selway, DNSc, CRNP
Adult/Pediatric Nurse Practitioner
Assistant Professor
University of Delaware
School of Nursing
Newark, Delaware

Lindsay Wilson, RN, MSN, CPNP
Pediatric Nurse Practitioner
Pediatric Gastroenterology and Nutrition
Johns Hopkins Children's Center
Johns Hopkins Hospital
Baltimore, Maryland

M. Elizabeth M. Younger, PhD, CPNP
Pediatric Immunology
Johns Hopkins Hospital
Baltimore, Maryland

1

Growth and Development

M. Elizabeth M. Younger

Select one best answer to the following questions.

1. H. O. is a 5-year-old Vietnamese child who has fallen off of his growth curve. The best intervention would be to:

   a. Suggest high-calorie breakfast drinks as supplements
   b. Incorporate traditional foods into a management plan that will provide increased calories and nutrients
   c. ⌣Educate the family on the need for increased calories and nutrients
   d. Refer family to growth clinic for evaluation

2. While taking the history of 6-month-old E. M., you learn that she is not sleeping through the night and will not fall back to sleep without the parents rocking or feeding her. This is an example of:

   a. Somnambulism
   b. Pavor nocturnus
   c. Learned behavior
   d. Delayed sleep phase

3. Which of the following scenarios is suggestive of a child who may not be ready to enter first grade? An inability to:

   a. Recognize six colors and remember one's phone number
   b. Accurately use pronouns
   c. Empathize with others
   d. Count to five and draw a person with three parts

4. T. T. is a 9-week-old preterm infant whose birth weight was 2.3 kg. Mom was HB_s Ag negative. He is seen today for the first time since discharge from the nursery. He has received no prior immunizations. The appropriate immunizations to give at this time would be:

   a. DTaP, Hib, IPV, rotavirus, Hep B-1, pneumococcal
   b. DTP, Hib, OPV, rotavirus, Hep B-1
   c. DTaP, Hib, rotavirus, IPV, pneumococcal
   d. DTaP, Hib, IPV, pneumococcal

5. While examining 10-year-old R. M.'s teeth you note that the upper incisors slightly overlap the lower incisors. The second and lower first molars are absent. Your assessment is:

   a. Malocclusion
   b. Delayed mandibular dentition
   c. Normal dentition
   d. Hyperdontia

6. The mother of 5-year-old D. W. is concerned that her son often cheats when playing board games with his older sister. What is the most appropriate response to D. W.'s behavior?

   a. Encourage the parent to use 5-minute time-outs when cheating occurs.
   b. Explain that D. W. is developmentally unable to comprehend rigid rules.
   c. Make sure that D. W. understands the rules before starting to play the game.
   d. Explain to D. W. that cheating is like lying and is not acceptable behavior.

7. Which of the following is not a sign of readiness to toilet train?

   a. Can sit for extended periods
   b. Can follow directions
   c. Occasional waking from naps with dry diapers
   d. Regularity of bowel movements

8. Which of the following physical findings in a 2-month-old child warrants an immediate referral to a neurologist/neurosurgeon?

   a. Head circumference growing faster than height and weight
   b. Unresolved cephalhematoma
   c. Rigid and immobile sagittal suture
   d. Snapping sensation when pressure is applied to parietal bone

9. While listening to 2.5-year-old K. L. talk, you note that she frequently omits final consonants and her sentences are two to three words in length. The appropriate plan of care would be:

   a. Routine follow-up at next well-child visit

   b. Referring for hearing screen
   c. Assessing for developmental delays
   d. Referring to a speech pathologist

10. The mother of 3-year-old G. W. reports that he has begun to stutter. Further probing reveals that the stuttering occurs frequently and lasts 1 to 2 seconds. G.W. does not seem bothered by the stuttering. The appropriate management would be:

    a. Referral to a speech pathologist
    b. Referral for an evaluation for an anxiety disorder
    c. Reassuring the mother that this is a mild problem
    d. Demonstrating to G. W. slow, deep breathing before talking

11. You would expect a school-age child to:

    a. Grow 1.5 inches per year
    b. Grow 0.5 inch per year
    c. Gain about 6 pounds per year
    d. Gain about 3 pounds per year

12. During 8-month-old L. B.'s physical examination, the father boasts that L. B. is going to be a left-handed batter since he prefers doing everything with his left hand. The appropriate response would be to:

    a. Ask if others in the family are left handed
    b. Suggest play activities that require using both hands
    c. Present toys more often to the right hand
    d. Perform a careful neurologic examination

13. At 12 years old, Peter has been diagnosed with constitutional growth delay. Appropriate management would include:

    a. Starting low-dose testosterone therapy now
    b. Counseling regarding delayed onset of puberty
    c. Thyroxine replacement
    d. Nutritional counseling

14. Which of the following best describes behavior associated with Piaget's concrete operations?

    a. Learning primarily by trial and error
    b. Interpreting events in relationship to themselves
    c. Categorizing information into lower to higher classes
    d. Drawing logical conclusions from observations

15. Jeffrey, at 8 years of age, has been diagnosed with ADHD and is receiving stimulant medication. Which of the following interventions would be least helpful?

    a. Monthly height and weight checks
    b. Small frequent meals and snacks
    c. High-calorie supplemental drinks
    d. Elimination of refined sugar from diet

16. The principle that growth and development becomes increasingly integrated is best demonstrated by:

    a. Gaining head control before raising the chest
    b. Bringing cup to mouth, tipping, and swallowing
    c. Rolling over before sitting
    d. Grasping with fist before using fingers

17. In males, Tanner Stage III can be distinguished from Tanner Stage II by:

    a. Fine, downy pubic hair at the base of penis
    b. Adultlike pubic hair not extending to thighs
    c. Penile growth in width
    d. Penile growth in length

18. T. J., 13 years old, reluctantly shares with you that his "chest hurts." On physical examination, you note unilateral breast enlargement, which is tender to palpation. You suspect physiologic gynecomastia. Which Tanner stage would support that diagnosis?

    a. Tanner stage I
    b. Tanner stage III

    c. Tanner Stage IV
    d. Tanner Stage V

19. During a physical examination of 10.5-year-old Melissa, you note the appearance of breast buds. You tell her that she can expect which of the following in approximately 2 years?

    a. Growth of pubic hair
    b. Peak height velocity
    c. Onset of menses
    d. Axillary hair

20. Adolescents who engage in risky behavior, such as driving without a seat belt, are displaying:

    a. A type of egocentrism
    b. A need for independence
    c. Role experimentation
    d. Low self-esteem

21. An increase in which of the following behaviors is seen more frequently in late, rather than in early, adolescence?

    a. Value conflict with parents
    b. Focus on physical appearance
    c. Peer group involvement
    d. Understanding inner motivations of others

◘ ANSWERS AND RATIONALE

1. **(b)** It is important for healthcare professionals to understand the cultural norms and perspectives of others. This often helps in compliance with suggestions for improved health. Asian families, out of respect, do not often ask questions or challenge advice. By understanding their food patterns and incorporating that into a diet plan, compliance may increase.

2. **(c)** Sleepwalking (somnambulism) and pavor nocturnus (night terrors) are sleep disturbances, which occur in school-age and preschool-age children respectively. Learned behavior is a result of parents interfering with the child's attempts to return to sleep without stimulation from the parents.

3. **(d)** Children entering first grade should have the requisite skills to master the tasks they will encounter. This includes language, fine and gross motor skills, and personal and social skills. At this age the child should be able to draw a person with at least six parts and count to 10 or more.

4. **(a)** Preterm infants should be immunized at the usual chronologic age with the regular doses. IPV should be given to avoid nosocomial transmission of polio virus vaccine strain.

5. **(b)** The mandibular (lower) molars usually erupt between ages 6 and 7. Even allowing for individual variation, this is a considerable delay. Hyperdontia refers to supernumerary teeth.

6. **(b)** Developmentally, the concept of cheating is not well understood until 7 years of age. The idea of playing fairly to assure everyone an equal chance occurs with maturity and the ability to differentiate among moral choices.

7. **(d)** Regularity of bowel movements is established early in infancy but has nothing to do with voluntary sphincter control necessary for toilet training.

8. **(c)** Ridged and immobile sutures indicate premature fusing resulting in craniosynostosis. For proper brain growth, sutures need to approximate each other yet remain mobile.

9. **(a)** Children aged 2 to 3 years have several articulation disfluencies, among them is the dropping of final consonants. Two- to three-word sentences are normal for the 24- to 30-month-old child.

10. **(c)** This represents a mild stuttering problem but does not warrant immediate referral unless the child or parent are increasingly concerned, or if it continues indefinitely.

11. **(c)** The recognized standard of physical growth of school-age children is to gain 5 to 7 pounds per year and grow about 2.5 inches per year.

12. **(d)** Handedness before a year is cause for concern and may indicate cerebral palsy. A neurologic examination is indicated. The examiner should carefully assess for increase in deep tendon reflexes and tone.

13. **(b)** Constitutional growth delay is considered a variant of normal marked by delayed onset of puberty, that is a delay in maturation. Laboratory studies are normal. Final growth is achieved later but is consistent with family genetics. Growth hormone r thyroxine is not recommended. Nutritional therapies will not change the outcome. Low-dose hormone therapy is appropriate for selected individuals with psychosocial concerns beginning at 14 years of age.

14. **(c)** Concrete operations occur during the school-age years as children begin to understand the characteristics of things and objects. Classification is a thought process that develops during this time.

15. **(d)** Stimulant medication may decrease the appetite, so, careful monitoring of growth and a nutritional plan that encourages adequate calories is important. There is no sound evidence that sugar or artificial additives play a role in ADHD.

16. **(b)** Infants must first develop hand–mouth coordination before incorporating tipping and swallowing, which is a more integrated function. Head control before raising the chest demonstrates the principle of cephalocaudal progression. Options "c" and "d" suggest proximal–distal progression.

17. **(d)** Most penile growth in Tanner Stage III is in length rather than width because of underdevelopment of the corpora cavernosa. Fine, downy pubic hair appears in Stage II and adultlike appearance occurs in Stage IV.

18. **(b)** Physiologic gynecomastia is a common clinical finding in young adolescent males. It is usually present during Tanner Stage III.

19. **(c)** Understanding the sequencing of pubertal development is important, but it must be remembered that individual timing may differ. In the female patient, pubic hair, axillary hair, and the peak height velocity generally occur before menarche.

20. **(a)** The belief that one is immune from poor or bad outcomes (e.g., death, disease) is a form of egocentrism known as personal fable in which adolescents believe that the laws of nature do not apply to them.

21. **(d)** Late adolescence is characterized by increased autonomy and beginning to appreciate the complexities and motivations of other people's behaviors.

◘ REFERENCES

American Academy of Family Physicians. (2008). *Growth and your newborn.* Available at: http://kidshealth.org/PageManager.jsp?dn=familydoctor&lic=44&cat_id=20052&article_set=21535&ps=104. Accessed January 17, 2010.

American Academy of Pediatrics. (1996). *The classification of child and adolescent mental diagnoses in primary care* (DSM-PC). Elk Grove, IL: American Academy of Pediatrics.

American Academy of Pediatrics. (2000). Clinical practice guidelines: Diagnosis and evaluation of the child with attention-deficit/hyperactivity disorder. *Pediatrics, 105,* 5, 1158–1170.

American Academy of Pediatrics. (2007). *Bright futures: Guidelines for health supervision of infants, children and adolescents.* Washington, DC: Author.

American Psychiatric Association. (2000). *Diagnostic and statistical manual of mental disorders—text revision* (4th ed.). Washington, DC: Author.

Behrman, R. E., Kliegman, R. M., & Jenson, H. B. (2002). *Nelson textbook of pediatrics* (17th ed.). Philadelphia, PA: W. B. Saunders Company.

Berger, K. S., & Straub, R. (2008). *The developing person through the life span* (7th ed.). New York, NY: Worth Publishers.

Burns, C. E., Dunn, A. M., Brady, M. A., Starr, N. B., & Blosser, C. (2008). *Pediatric primary care: A handbook for nurse practitioners* (4th ed.). Philadelphia, PA: W. B. Saunders Company.

Child Welfare Information Gateway. (2008). *Child abuse and neglect fatalities: Statistics and interventions.* Available at: http://www.childwelfare.gov/pubs/factsheets/fatality.cfm. Accessed August 19, 2009.

Daniels, S. R., Greer, F. R., & the Committee on Nutrition. (2008). Lipid screening and cardiovascular health in children. *Pediatrics, 122,* 1, 198–208.

Dixon, S. D., & Stein, M. T. (2005). *Encounters with children: Pediatric behavior and development* (4th ed.). St. Louis, MO: Mosby Year Book, Inc.

Dopheide, J. A., & Pliszka, S. R. (2009). Attention-deficit-hyperactivity disorder: An update. *Pharmacotherapy, 29,* 6, 656–679.

Feldman, H. M., Coleman, W. L., Carey, W. B., & Crocker, A. C. (2009). *Developmental-behavioral pediatrics* (4th ed.). Philadelphia, PA: WB Saunders.

Findling, R. L. (2008). Evolution of the treatment of attention-deficit/hyperactivity disorder in children: A review. *Clinical Therapeutics, 30,* 5, 942–957.

Genel, M., McCaffree, M. A., Hendricks, K., Dennery, P. A., Hay, W. W., Jr., Stanton, B., Szilagyi, P. G., & Jenkins, R. R. (2008). A national agenda for America's children and adolescents in 2008: Recommendations from the 15th annual public policy plenary symposium, annual meeting of the

Pediatric Academic Societies, May 3, 2008. *Pediatrics, 122*, 4, 843–849.

Hanson, S. M. H., & Boyde, S. T. (2001). *Family health care nursing: Theory, practice and research*. Philadelphia, PA: R. A. Davis.

Hoekelman, R. A., Adam, H. M., Nelson, N. M., Weitzman, M. L., & Wilson, M. H. (2001). *Primary pediatric care* (4th ed.). St. Louis, MO: Mosby Year Book, Inc.

Johnson, C. P., Myers, S. M., & American Academy of Pediatrics Council on Children with Disabilities. (2007). Identification and evaluation of children with autism spectrum disorders. *Pediatrics, 120*, 5, 1183–1215.

McGough, J. J., & McCracken, J. T. (2000). Assessment of attention deficit hyperactivity disorder: A review of recent literature. *Current Opinions in Pediatrics, 12*, 4, 319–324.

McMillan, J. (2006). *Oski's pediatrics: Principles and practice* (4th ed.). Philadelphia, PA: Lippincott, Williams & Wilkins.

Myers, S. M., Johnson, C. P., & American Academy of Pediatrics Council on Children with Disabilities. (2007). Management of children with autism spectrum disorders. *Pediatrics, 120*, 5, 1162–1182.

Neinstein, L. S., Gordon, C. M., Katzman, D. K., Rosen, D. S., & Woods, E. R. (Eds.). (2007). *Adolescent health care: A practical guide* (5th ed.). Philadelphia, PA: Lippincott, Williams & Wilkins.

Shonkoff, J. P., & Phillips, D. A. (2000). *From neurons to neighborhoods: The science of early childhood development*. Washington, DC: National Academy Press.

Simkin, D. R. (2002). Adolescent substance abuse disorders and comorbidity. *Pediatric Clinics of North America, 49*, 2, 463–477.

Stirling, J., Jr., & American Academy of Pediatrics Committee on Child Abuse and Neglect. (2007). Beyond Munchausen syndrome by proxy: Identification and treatment of child abuse in a medical setting. *Pediatrics, 119*, 5, 1026–1030.

Substance Abuse and Mental Health Services Administration (SAMHSA) (2006). *Results from the 2005 National Survey on Drug Use and Health: National Findings*. Rockville, MD: Substance Abuse and Mental Health Services Administration Office of Applied Studies.

US Department of Health and Human Services, Administration on Children, Youth and Families. (2007) *Child maltreatment 2007*. Washington, DC: US Government Printing Office.

US Department of Health and Human Services. (2001). *Child maltreatment 2001: Reports from the states to the national child abuse and neglect data system*. Washington, DC: US Government Printing Office.

US Department of Health and Human Services. (1998). *Clinician's handbook of preventive services* (2nd ed.). Washington, DC: US Government Printing Office.

US Department of Health and Human Services. (2005). *Healthy People: 2010*. Washington, DC: US Government Printing Office. Available at: http://www.healthypeople.gov. Accessed January 17, 2010.

US Preventative Services Task Force (2008). Universal screening for hearing loss in infants: US Preventative Task Force recommendation statement. *Pediatrics, 122*, 1, 143–148.

Zero to Three. (2005). *Diagnostic classification: 0–3: Diagnostic classification of mental health and developmental disorders of infancy and early childhood*. Washington, DC: Zero to Three.

Health Promotion and Maintenance

JoAnne Silbert-Flagg

Select one best answer to the following questions.

1. You detect a heart murmur while examining a 3-year-old child. In determining whether or not a referral is necessary, you determine it is an "innocent" heart murmur for which of the following reasons?

   a. It is best heard during diastole.
   b. It radiates to the axilla.
   c. The intensity is no greater than I or II/VI.
   d. There is no variation with change in child's position.

2. When providing anticipatory guidance about infant development, you might teach parents that a normal infant could first transfer an object from hand to hand at which age?

   a. 2 months
   b. 4 months
   c. 7 months
   d. 9 months

3. A 2-month-old infant at your clinic received a combined DTaP/HepB/IPV vaccine and the parents are in need of teaching about possible side effects. Which of the following is not an adverse effect following administration of the DTaP vaccination?

   a. Local reaction
   b. Fever
   c. Increased fussiness
   d. Transient morbilliform rash

4. When reviewing immunization protocols at your clinic, you are aware that the varicella vaccine can be administered to susceptible children beginning at what age?

   a. 4 months
   b. 6 months
   c. 12 months
   d. 15 months

5. A 2-week-old infant is in the clinic for a scheduled weight check. The best indication that a 2-week-old infant is receiving adequate breastmilk is that the baby:

   a. Passes at least four stools per day
   b. Feeds every three hours
   c. Voids four times a day
   d. Has regained birthweight

6. A mother of an 8-month-old infant asks you for advice about continued introduction of solids. Which of the following food groups do you recommend be introduced to the baby last?

   a. Egg yolk
   b. Egg white
   c. Fruits
   d. Vegetables

7. The mother of a 15-month-old child informs you that she feeds the baby skim milk. You advise the mother to change to whole milk primarily because skim milk:

   a. Is not as easily digested as whole milk
   b. Contains an insufficient amount of calcium
   c. Contains too little protein
   d. Provides an inadequate amount of essential fatty acids

8. An adolescent is being evaluated for childhood depression. Which behavior or sign is least likely to be evident?

   a. Evidence of hallucinations and delusions
   b. A history of recurrent "accidents"
   c. A sense of guilt
   d. The presence of eating disorders

9. A 12-year-old boy is brought into the clinic for an urgent visit after having ingested 10 diazepam tablets. Following the initial emergent care and stabilization of the child, the most important aspect of your management is:

   a. Referring the case to the social services
   b. Assessing the family supports available to the child
   c. Obtaining a psychiatric consultation
   d. Reviewing the history for signs of depression

10. You are seeing a 15-month-old boy with leukemia for a check-up. If indicated, this child may receive all of the following vaccines except:

   a. Inactivated polio vaccine (IPV)
   b. *H. influenzae* type B (Hib)
   c. Diphtheria, tetanus, acellular pertussis (DTaP)
   d. Varicella (VAR)

11. While conducting the Denver II developmental screening test, the mother of an 18-month-old child reports to you that the toddler does not imitate activities. You decide to assess the child's development further by giving him tasks from which sector?

   a. Personal–social
   b. Fine motor–adaptive
   c. Language
   d. Gross motor

12. You have ordered routine blood screening for a 2-year-old girl who, because of dietary habits, is at risk for iron deficiency anemia. Which of the following findings is not associated with iron deficiency anemia?

   a. Hypochromic RBC
   b. Microcytic RBC
   c. Low reticulocyte count
   d. Low free erythrocyte protoporphyrin (FEP) level

13. During a prenatal visit, you review the mother's record for routine prenatal screening results. While educating the mother, you explain that the screening of maternal serum for alpha-fetoprotein (MSAFP) between the 15th and 21st weeks of pregnancy is done primarily to screen for:

   a. Phenylketonuria
   b. Galactosemia
   c. Cystic fibrosis
   d. Neural tube defects

14. A tenderness is detected over the tibial tuberosity of a 10-year-old boy during a routine examination at a school-based clinic. The PNP knows this may be a sign of:

   a. Osgood-Schlatter disease
   b. Blount's disease
   c. Plantar fasciitis
   d. Effusion in the joint space

15. The parents of a 1-week-old infant are concerned about the unusual shape of their child's head. In the physical examination of the infant, which of the following signs would not support a diagnosis of craniosynostosis?

    a. Palpation of a ridge along a given suture line
    b. Unusual skull configuration
    c. A palpable lesion at the occipital region
    d. Abnormal head circumference

16. In the emergency room, you encounter a toddler whose injuries are not consistent with the history that is given. Which of the following would be the best step a provider could take in order to foster communication with abusive parents?

    a. Realize that abusive parents have essentially different goals for their children than other caregivers do
    b. Understand that parental hostility and resistance are potent symptoms of fear and inadequacy
    c. Consider referring the parents to a substance abuse program
    d. Be cautious when sharing the results of medical findings

17. You are preparing a drug prevention program for middle school students. Your educational approach is based on the knowledge that the most common substance of abuse in adolescence is:

    a. Marijuana
    b. Cocaine
    c. Heroin
    d. Alcohol

18. During a check-up of a 15-month-old girl, you note that the child has dropped significantly in percentile for weight over the past few months. In evaluating a child with failure to thrive, the most important part of your assessment involves:

    a. The history
    b. The physical examination
    c. Laboratory studies
    d. Observation of family interactions

19. A 7-year-old child in your caseload has recently been placed on methylphenidate for behavioral concerns associated with ADHD. Which of the following side effects are not associated with this drug?

    a. Decreased appetite
    b. Weight loss
    c. Irritability
    d. Decreased heart rate

20. The parents of an 8-year-old child are concerned that their son does not want to attend school. Which of the following historical findings are not usually associated with the diagnosis of school phobia?

    a. Sporadic school absence
    b. Chronic medical illness
    c. Vague physical symptoms
    d. Depression and anxiety

21. A 17-year-old girl is referred to your clinic by the school nurse to be assessed for an eating disorder. Which of the following dynamics is not characteristic of anorexia nervosa?

    a. Excessive eating followed by purging
    b. A pervasive sense of helplessness and ineffectiveness
    c. Weight loss that gives the patient a sense of mastery and control
    d. Low body temperature, pulse rate, and blood pressure

◘ ANSWERS AND RATIONALE

1. **(c)** Innocent murmurs usually have an intensity of no greater than I or II/VI, occur early in systole, are not likely to radiate over parts of the chest, and the presence and intensity vary with change in the child's position.

2. **(c)** A normal infant transfers objects from hand to hand by 7 months of age.

3. **(d)** A transient morbilliform rash is an adverse effect associated with the MMR vaccine.

4. **(c)** According to the recommended Childhood Immunization Schedule approved by the ACIP and AAP, the varicella vaccine can be administered at 12 months of age.

5. **(d)** The newborn may lose 7 to 10% of birthweight the first three days and then should gain 0.5 to 1 ounce a day and regain birthweight by 2 weeks of age.

6. **(b)** Rice cereal, the least allergenic of cereals, should be offered first, followed by fruits and vegetables, meats, egg yolk, and egg white.

7. **(d)** All milk (human and cow) is deficient in iron. Skim milk should be avoided until 2 years of age because it provides too few calories, an excess of protein, and an inadequate amount of essential fatty acids.

8. **(a)** Hallucinations and delusions are uncommon in the presentation of adolescent depression.

9. **(c)** Every actively suicidal patient, regardless of apparent seriousness, requires psychiatric consultation and, in some cases, hospitalization.

10. **(d)** Children with cancer and children receiving high-dose corticosteroids or other immunosuppressive agents should not be immunized with live virus or live bacteria vaccines.

11. **(a)** Imitating activities is considered to be a personal–social task.

12. **(d)** Iron deficiency anemia is a microcytic, hypochromic anemia associated with a low reticulocyte count and elevated FEP level.

13. **(d)** The MSAFP is used primarily to screen for neural tube defects. The other diseases are usually screened for at birth.

14. **(a)** Tenderness over the tibial tubercle may be a sign of Osgood-Schlatter disease. Blount's disease is characterized by severe bowing of the legs, and plantar fasciitis is associated with painful heels.

15. **(c)** Diagnosis of craniosynostosis is suspected as a result of skull configuration, a ridge along a suture line, and abnormal head circumference. Other palpable lesions, which often occur in the occipital region, are not indicative of craniosynostosis.

16. **(b)** Parental fear and inadequacy may be manifested as hostility. Abusive parents generally have similar goals for their children as others and are not any more likely to be substance abusers than nonabusive parents. Medical findings should be shared with the parents (without necessarily promoting an etiologic conclusion).

17. **(d)** Alcohol is the most common substance of abuse consumed by teenagers.

18. **(a)** The two major causes of poor growth, inadequate intake and social problems, are detected through the history.

19. **(d)** A common side effect of stimulants is a small increase in heart rate or blood pressure.

20. **(b)** Children with chronic medical illness typically strive actively to remain in school. The findings listed in the other answer choices are more likely to be associated with school phobia.

21. **(a)** Excessive eating followed by purging is a sign of bulimia.

◘ REFERENCES

Alaria, A. J., & Birnkrant, J. D. (Eds.). (2008). *Practical guide to the care of the pediatric patient* (2nd ed.). Philadelphia, PA: Mosby Elsevier.

Academy of Breastfeeding Medicine. (2008). *Academy of breastfeeding medicine.* Available at: http://www.bfmed.org. Accessed June 29, 2009.

Pickering L. K., Baker C. J., Kimberlin D. W., & Long S. S. (Eds.). (2009). *Red book online.* Available at: http://aapredbook.aappublications.org/. Accessed June 29, 2009.

American Academy of Pediatrics Policy Statement. (2008). Red reflex examination in neonates, infants and children. *Pediatrics, 122,* 6, 1401–1404.

Center for Disease Control and Prevention. (2009). *Vaccines and immunizations.* Available at: http://www.cdc.gov/vaccines/recs/schedules/default.htm. Accessed June 29, 2009.

Custer, J.W., & Rau, R. E. (Eds.). (2009). *The Harriet Lane handbook* (18th ed.). St. Louis, MO: Mosby.

Daniels, S. R., Greer, F. R., & the Committee on Nutrition. (2008). Lipid screening and cardiovascular health in children. *American Academy of Pediatrics, 122,* 1, 198–208.

Hagan, J. F., Shaw, J. S., & Duncan, P. M. (Eds.). (2008). *Bright futures: Guidelines for health supervision of infants, children and adolescents.* Elk Grove Village, IL: American Academy of Pediatrics.

Hale, T. W. (2008). *Medications and mothers' milk* (13th ed.). Amarillo, TX: Hale Publishing.

Hay, W. W., Haywood, A. R., Levin, M. J., & Sondheimer, J. M. (Eds.). (2009). *Current pediatric diagnosis & treatment* (19th ed.). Stamford, CT: McGraw-Hill/ Appleton & Lange.

National Institutes of Health & National Heart, Lung, and Blood Institute. (2005). *Fourth report on the diagnosis, evaluation, and treatment of high blood pressure in children and adolescents.* Available at: http://www.nhlbi.nih.gov/guidelines/hypertension/child_tbl.htm. Accessed June 29, 2009.

Nice, F. J. (2007). *Nonprescription drugs for the breastfeeding mother.* Amarillo, TX: Hale Publishing.

Rice, S. G., & The Council on Sports Medicine and Fitness. (2008). Medical conditions affecting sports participation. *Pediatrics, 121,* 4, 841–847.

Seidel, H. M., Rosenstein, B. J., Pathak, A., & McKay, W. H. (Eds.). (2006). *Primary care of the newborn* (4th ed.). Philadelphia, PA: Saunders Elsevier.

Schanler, R. J. (Ed.). (2006). *Breastfeeding handbook for physicians.* Elk Grove Village, IL: American Academy of Pediatrics & American College of Obstetricians and Gynecologists.

Vaccine Adverse Event Reporting System. (2009). *Vaccine adverse event reporting system.* Available at: http://vaers.hhs.gov/. Accessed June 29, 2009.

Ear, Eye, Nose, and Throat Disorders

Elizabeth Sloand and JoAnne Silbert-Flagg

Select one best answer to the following questions.

1. Following an episode of meningitis, it is most important to assess the child for:

   a. Hearing loss
   b. Changes in taste
   c. Cervical lymphadenopathy
   d. Tinnitus

2. An 8-year-old boy has been brought to the clinic with a chief complaint of ear pain. When you grasp the pinna of the ear, he says "that hurts real bad." These findings are consistent with a diagnosis of:

   a. Serous otitis media
   b. Mastoiditis
   c. Otitis externa
   d. Cholesteatoma

3. Steven, at 10 years of age, has been diagnosed with otitis externa twice this year. Health teaching for Steven and his mother should include:

   a. Emphasis on consistent use of low-dose prophylactic antibiotics
   b. Sleeping with the affected ear in the dependent position
   c. Information on the use of decongestants to open the eustachian tube
   d. Information on the use of acetic acid after ear canal contact with water

4. Following tympanostomy tube insertion, it is important that the tubes remain patent. Which of the following methods may be used to determine patency?

   a. Visual inspection
   b. Impedance tympanometry
   c. Valsalva maneuver
   d. Instillation of an ototopical suspension

5. The diagnosis of acute otitis media in a 1-year-old child is based on:

   a. Abnormal findings when pneumatic otoscopy and hearing test are performed
   b. Changes in the tympanic membrane's contour, color, and mobility
   c. Presence of fever and color of the tympanic membrane
   d. Presence of fever, ear pain, and tenderness of the pinna

6. Connor, 12 months of age, has been treated five times for acute otitis media. When planning Conner's follow-up care, it is most important to evaluate for which of the following?

   a. Otitis externa
   b. Hearing loss
   c. Enlarged tonsils
   d. Shotty lymph nodes

7. Brian, who is 13 years old, presents to the clinic with a sore throat. History reveals that he had a sore throat a couple of weeks ago and thought he had gotten well. He now has severe pharyngeal pain of 2 days duration and says he has been sweating and thinks he has fever. Physical examination reveals a temperature of 102°F and erythematous and edematous pharynx and soft palate. The right tonsil is swollen and inflamed without exudate and the uvula is displaced to the left. Right cervical nodes are tender. Lungs are clear to auscultation. Brian's signs and symptoms are suggestive of:

   a. Acute uvulitis
   b. Viral pharyngitis
   c. Epiglottitis
   d. Peritonsillar abscess

8. Which of the following is an expected finding after treatment of acute suppurative otitis media?

   a. Otitis externa
   b. Central auditory dysfunction
   c. Functional hearing loss
   d. Middle ear effusion

9. The mother of 2-year-old Shanda has brought her to the clinic because she thinks the child is having trouble hearing. Your evaluation of the complaint should start with:

   a. Asking detailed questions related to Shanda's medical history
   b. Examination of the ear
   c. Tympanometry and hearing tests
   d. Assuring the mother that transient hearing loss in childhood is common

10. Assessment of the red reflex may be used to rule out which of the following?

    a. Opacities
    b. Myopia or hyperopia
    c. Decreased visual acuity
    d. Blindness

11. The mother of 2-year-old Bridget has brought her to the clinic because "she got bathroom cleanser in her eye." History reveals that about 30 minutes ago, Bridget was sitting on the floor playing with a squeeze bottle of bathroom cleaner, when the bottle accidentally opened and the liquid splashed into her right eye. Physical examination reveals a reddened right eye with an edematous lid. Initial treatment should include:

    a. Allowing the natural tearing process to cleanse the eye
    b. Performing a retinal fundoscopic examination to assess for burns
    c. Irrigating the eye with copious amount of normal saline
    d. Referring Bridget to an ophthalmologist

12. The mother of a 5-year-old boy has brought him to the clinic because she thinks he has pinkeye. Which of the following would lead you to consider a diagnosis other than bacterial conjunctivitis?

    a. Hyperemic conjunctiva
    b. Scratchy sensation in the eye
    c. Decreased corneal clarity
    d. Copious tearing

13. Julie, at 18 months of age, has been brought to the clinic by her mother who tells you that Julie has had a cold for the past four days. There is no history of cough and the mother is unsure whether Julie has had fever. Physical examination reveals greenish, blood-tinged mucus with a strong, foul odor, draining from the right nostril. This clinical picture is most consistent with a diagnosis of:

    a. Allergic rhinitis
    b. Viral rhinitis
    c. Acute sinusitis
    d. Nasal foreign body

14. In a child with chronic sinusitis, the most accurate method of identifying sinus abnormalities is:

    a. Dark room transillumination of the sinuses
    b. Percussion of the paranasal sinuses
    c. AP, lateral, and occipitomental sinus radiographs
    d. CT scan of the sinuses

Questions 15 and 16 refer to the following scenario.

Mike, at 10 years of age, has been brought to the clinic with a cold. History reveals that he has had a runny nose and cough for about 10 days. There is no history of frequent respiratory problems. Physical examination reveals a temperature of 100° F and edematous cervical lymph nodes. Eyes are without redness or swelling. Examination of the nose is significant for mucopurulent drainage from the middle meatus bilaterally. The pharynx is erythematous without tonsillar enlargement or exudate. Breath is malodorous and lungs are clear to auscultation.

15. Mike's management should include:

    a. Culture of the nasal drainage
    b. Radiograph of the sinuses
    c. Measurement of erythrocyte sedimentation rate
    d. Use of an antibiotic

16. Two days after Mike's first visit, his mother brings him back to the clinic because he has a "swollen eye." Observation reveals redness and inflammation of the right eyelid with impaired extraocular movement. Which action is appropriate?

    a. Reassure the mother that this is a common and usually benign condition
    b. Treat Mike for bacterial conjunctivitis
    c. Order anti-inflammatory eye drops
    d. Refer Mike immediately to emergency room

17. The mother of 12-year-old Nathan has brought him to the clinic because he has had a runny nose for 2 weeks. History reveals that Nathan has visited the clinic three other times this year for upper respiratory complaints. Examination reveals slightly edematous and erythematous eyes, pale nasal mucosa with clear mucus, and pharynx with thin secretions posteriorly. There is no tonsillar swelling or exudate. Lips and nail beds are pink. Lymph node examination is significant for multiple shotty nodes. Lungs are clear to auscultation. Which action is appropriate at this time?

    a. Discuss symptomatic relief of the common cold with Nathan and his mother
    b. Culture nasal drainage and delay treatment until results are known
    c. Order an antibiotic
    d. Order an antihistamine

18. A 1-week-old infant has been diagnosed with nasolacrimal duct obstruction. A typical initial therapy includes:

    a. Use of prophylactic oral antibiotics
    b. Nasolacrimal sac massage
    c. Surgical opening of obstructed ducts
    d. Referral to an ophthalmologist

19. Marie, at 4 years old, has been brought to the clinic because she "has something wrong with her eye." Marie and her mother report that there has been no injury to the eye and that it has been red since yesterday. Examination reveals conjunctival hyperemia and a copious amount of purulent discharge bilaterally. Vision, pupillary reflexes, and corneal clarity are all normal. Which treatment should be ordered?

    a. Sodium sulfacetamide ophthalmic solution
    b. Gentamycin ophthalmic solution
    c. Tobramycin ophthalmic solution
    d. Cromolyn sodium ophthalmic solution

20. During the routine examination of a 12-year-old boy, you detect a group of hard, fixed, nontender lymph nodes, each of which measure about 1 centimeter, in the posterior cervical chain. You are unable to detect any signs of infection. Your management should include:

    a. Recording the finding and reassessing the nodes in 1 month
    b. Ordering a 10-day course of a broad spectrum antibiotic and reevaluating the nodes in 2 weeks
    c. Ordering a CBC, erythrocyte sedimentation rate, and chest radiograph
    d. Referring the child to an allergist

21. Which method might be used to assess the vision of a 1-month-old child?

    a. Check the vessel pattern of the fundus of the eye
    b. Watch to see if the infant turns his or her head toward you when you speak
    c. Observe the pattern of interaction with the mother
    d. Perform the Titmus test on the infant

◘ ANSWERS AND RATIONALE

1. **(a)** Complications of meningitis include hydrocephalus, deafness, and blindness.

2. **(c)** With otitis externa, exquisite tenderness is noted when pressure is placed on the tragus or pinna of the ear.

3. **(d)** Otitis externa can be prevented by instilling 2% acetic acid (half-strength vinegar) in the external auditory canal after ear canal contact with water. Half isopropyl alcohol can also be used.

4. **(a)** Visual inspection is used to determine tube patency.

5. **(b)** The diagnosis of acute otitis media is based on changes in the contour, color, and mobility of the tympanic membrane. Redness of the tympanic membrane alone can be caused by crying and is not a reliable sign of acute otitis media. Changes in contour, mobility, and hearing may be caused by nonsuppurative or serous otitis media. Fever, ear pain, and tenderness of the pinna may indicate otitis externa.

6. **(b)** Hearing loss is the most common complication of otitis media. Children who have multiple infections should have their hearing assessed. Tonsils are normally large in young children. Shotty lymph nodes are usually associated with past infections and are not clinically significant.

7. **(d)** This presentation is classical for peritonsillar abscess, which is generally treated with incision and drainage and antibiotics.

8. **(d)** Middle ear effusion (serous otitis media) is frequently seen after acute otitis media. Central auditory dysfunction is caused by the brain's inability to use sound properly. Functional hearing loss means there is no disturbance with any organ and may be psychiatric in origin.

9. **(a)** The investigation of all complaints begins with exploration of the history. Hearing loss in childhood is extremely common. Specific historic risk factors for hearing loss are family history of congenital hearing loss, prenatal or perinatal infection, birth trauma or anoxia, and use of aminoglycosides.

10. **(a)** A normal red reflex rules out opacities, intraocular tumor, and coloboma. The red reflex does not assess visual acuity. A nonvisible red reflex indicates obstruction in the preretinal chambers.

11. **(c)** Acid or alkali chemical eye injuries are acute emergencies and require copious normal saline. Overirrigation is not a problem, but litmus paper can be used to determine when the chemical has been neutralized. The child should be referred to an ophthalmologist after irrigation of the eye.

12. **(c)** Bacterial conjunctivitis does not affect corneal clarity. A more serious condition should be suspected (such as keratitis, corneal ulcer, or glaucoma) and the child should be referred to an ophthalmologist if the cornea is not clear.

13. **(d)** Nasal foreign body is characterized by unilateral purulent discharge that may be blood tinged. Nasal discharge is very foul smelling. Allergic rhinitis and viral rhinitis usually cause clear bilateral nasal secretions, while sinusitis usually produces bilateral drainage with less odor.

14. **(d)** CT scans are superior to sinus radiographs in the identification of abnormalities. A normal radiograph suggests, but does not prove, that sinuses are free of disease.

15. **(d)** The signs and symptoms, especially mucopurulent drainage from the middle meatus, are supportive of a diagnosis of acute sinusitis. Sinus radiographs are difficult to interpret and not indicated at this time. Culture of nasal drainage is not useful in the determination of the causative organism in sinusitis. There are no signs of complications, and it is appropriate to treat the condition with antibiotics.

16. **(d)** History of sinusitis often precedes orbital cellulitis. Examination indicates that Mike may have orbital cellulitis, a medical emergency that requires hospitalization and IV antibiotics. He should be referred to the emergency room.

17. **(d)** Repeated episodes of upper respiratory illness, clear nasal secretions, and pale nasal mucosa are common in children with allergies. Antihistamines are used to treat seasonal and perennial allergies.

18. **(b)** Nasolacrimal sac massage using downward strokes raises the pressure in the nasolacrimal sac and may overcome the obstruction. Topical ophthalmic antibiotic may be indicated. Early surgical opening of the ducts may be performed to relieve parental anxiety, but conservative treatment is successful by 1 year of age in about 90% of cases. Referral to an ophthalmologist is indicated if the condition persists beyond 6 months or is frequently purulent.

19. **(a)** Marie's presentation supports a diagnosis of bacterial conjunctivitis. Sodium sulfacetamide, erythromycin, or polymixin B sulfate-trimethoprim sulfate solution are appropriate first-line treatments. Gentamycin and tobramycin should be reserved for suspected gram-negative bacterial conjunctivitis or when justified by culture results. Cromolyn sodium is used to treat allergic conjunctivitis.

20. **(c)** Nodes that are matted, hard, fixed, and nontender are characteristic of cancer. Lymph nodes associated with Hodgkin's disease usually begin in the lower cervical area. A chest radiograph, CBC, and erythrocyte sedimentation rate should be obtained in any patient with lymphadenopathy that is atypical for infection.

21. **(c)** Nonquantitative, but clinically helpful information may be gained about the infant's vision by observing whether or not the infant fixates on and attempts to follow the mother's face.

◻ REFERENCES

Behrman, R., Kliegman, R., & Jenson, H. (2007). *Nelson textbook of pediatrics*. Philadelphia, PA: Saunders.

Bernius, M., & Perlin, D. (2006). Pediatric ear, nose and throat emergencies. *Pediatric Clinics of North America, 53*, 2, 195–214.

Bord, S., & Linden, J. (2008). Trauma to the globe and orbit. *Emergency Medical Clinics of North America, 26*, 1, 97–123.

Chayavichitsilp, P., Buckwalter, J.V., Krakowski, A.C., & Friedlander, S.F. (2009). Herpes simplex. *Pediatrics in Review 30*, 4, 119–129.

Choby, B. (2009). Diagnosis and treatment of streptococcal pharyngitis. *American Family Physician, 79,* 5, 383–389.

Custer, J. W., & Rau, R. E. (Eds.). (2009). *The Harriet Lane handbook* (18th ed.). St. Louis, MO: Elsevier.

Edmondson, N., & Parikh, S. (2008). Complications of acute bacterial sinusitis in children. *Pediatric Annals, 37,* 10, 680–685.

Friedmann, A. (2008). Evaluation and management of lymphadenopathy in children. *Pediatrics in Review, 29,* 2, 53–59.

Greenberg, M., & Pollard, Z. (2003). The red eye in childhood. *Pediatric Clinics of North America, 50,* 1, 105–124.

Goldsmith, A., & Rosendeld, R. (2003). Treatment of pediatric sinusitis. *Pediatric Clinics of North America, 50,* 1, 413–426.

Hay, W., Levin, M., Sondheimer, J., & Deterding, R. (2009). *Current diagnosis and treatment pediatrics.* New York, NY: McGraw-Hill.

Jaggi, P. (2006). Group A streptococcal infections. *Pediatrics in Review, 27,* 3, 99–104.

Kliegman, R., Greenbaum, L., & Lye, P. (2004). *Practical strategies in pediatric diagnosis and therapy.* Philadelphia, PA: Elsevier Saunders.

Krol, D. (2007). Oral conditions. *Pediatrics in Review, 28,* 1, 15–20.

Levine, L. (2003). Pediatric ocular trauma and shaken infant syndrome. *Pediatric Clinics in North America, 50,* 1, 137–148.

Majumdar, S., & Bateman, N. (2009). Diagnosis and management of otalgia in children. *Archives of Disease in Childhood Education & Practice, 94, 38,* 33–36.

McCann, D., Worsfold, S., Mullee, M., Petrou, S., Stevenson, J., & Yuen, H. (2009). Reading and communication skills after universal newborn screening for permanent childhood hearing impairment. *Archives of Diseases of Children, 94,* 4, 293–297.

Paradise, J., & Bluestone, C. (2005). Tympanostomy tubes: A contemporary guide to judicious use. *Pediatrics in Review, 26,* 2, 61–66.

Prentiss, K., & Dorfman, D. (2008). Pediatric ophthalmology in the emergency department. *Emergency Medical Clinics of North America, 26,* 1, 181–198.

Rafei, K., & Lichenstein, R. (2006). Airway infectious disease emergencies. *Pediatric Clinics of North America, 53,* 2, 215–242.

Stone, K. (2007). Otitis externa. *Pediatrics in Review, 28,* 2, 77–78.

Schwartz, M. (2005). *The 5-minute pediatric consult.* Philadelphia, PA: Lippincott, Williams & Wilkins.

Zitelli, B., & Davis, H. (2007). *Atlas of pediatric physical diagnosis.* Philadelphia, PA: Mosby Elsevier.

4

Cardiovascular Disorders

Peggy Dorr

Select one best answer to the following questions.

1. The most common congenital heart defect (CHD) in children is:

   a. Tricuspid atresia
   b. Ventricular septal defect
   c. Coarctation of the aorta
   d. Pulmonary atresia with intact ventricular septum

2. The mother of a 4-month-old infant reports that he turned "blue" and seemed to have fast, labored breathing after vigorous crying soon after awakening. He settled down and his color and breathing seemed to improve. On physical examination, the mucous membranes of the lips and mouth appear mildly cyanotic. A systolic murmur is heard best at the left sternal border. Vital signs are normal with normal peripheral pulses. There is no hepatomegaly. A likely diagnosis is:

   a. Congestive heart failure
   b. Acute life-threatening event related to reflux
   c. Coarctation of the aorta
   d. Cyanotic spell related to tetralogy of Fallot

3. Management of the infant with suspected heart disease and a reported cyanotic spell should include:

   a. Prompt referral to a cardiologist
   b. An apnea monitor for 30 days to document further events
   c. Instructing the parent to keep a diary of these episodes
   d. Continuous administration of oxygen

4. Chest pain in young children is usually:

   a. A symptom of congenital heart disease
   b. Noncardiac in origin
   c. An early sign of hypercholesterolemia
   d. A symptom of congestive heart failure

5. A common cause of congestive heart failure in the first year of life is:

   a. Mild pulmonary stenosis
   b. Inflammatory heart disease
   c. Rheumatic fever
   d. Complete heart block

6. The least likely physical finding in a 2-month-old infant with congestive heart failure is:

   a. Tachypnea
   b. Tachycardia
   c. Hepatomegaly
   d. Pedal edema

7. Which of the following may cause volume overload leading to congestive heart failure (CHF) if not appropriately followed and managed?

   a. Coarctation of the aorta
   b. Pulmonary stenosis
   c. Ventricular septal defect
   d. Supraventricular tachycardia

8. A vibratory systolic murmur is heard between the lower left sternal border and the apex in a healthy 4-year-old girl at her preschool physical. There are no concerns from the parent. The cardiovascular exam is otherwise normal. A likely diagnosis is:

   a. Venous hum
   b. Still's murmur
   c. Transposition of the great arteries
   d. Rheumatic heart disease

9. Characteristics of a venous hum include:

   a. A systolic murmur
   b. Radiation over precordium
   c. Marked decrease or disappearance of murmur when child is supine
   d. Heard best at lower left sternal border

10. Which of the following is true regarding innocent murmurs?

    a. The murmur is often holosystolic.
    b. Prompt referral to a cardiologist is indicated.
    c. A precordial thrill is present.
    d. The murmur is low in intensity, grade 1 through 3.

11. SBE prophylaxis is recommended for:

    a. All children with congenital heart disease on a daily basis
    b. All children with congenital heart disease before dental, GI, and GU procedures
    c. Children with repaired congenital heart disease with a residual defect at the repair site
    d. Children who have undergone surgical repair of a congenital heart condition, for 5 years after procedure

12. A 12-year-old girl seen at a routine visit has a blood pressure of 145/90. She denies any symptoms. The initial management would include:

    a. Intravenous pyelogram
    b. Return for two repeat blood pressure measurements
    c. No follow-up needed—blood pressure probably related to anxiety
    d. Diuretic therapy

13. A 4-year-old Caucasian female presents for a well-child check. Her blood pressure by auscultation is 135/80. There is no significant family history of hypertension or heart disease. Besides wanting to repeat the blood pressures for accuracy, what are potential differential diagnoses for this child?

    a. Severe coronary artery disease
    b. Renal artery stenosis and coarctation of the aorta
    c. Rheumatic fever and ventricular septal defect
    d. Tetralogy of Fallot and coarctation of the aorta

14. A 9-year-old boy presents with a fever of 102°F and complains of leg pains. His mother reports that he had an upper respiratory infection with a sore throat approximately 2 weeks ago, which subsided without therapy. On physical examination, he has tender, swollen knees bilaterally. His heart rate is 120/min and a blowing systolic murmur is heard at the apex that was not noted on previous visits. The most likely diagnosis is:

    a. Kawasaki disease
    b. Rheumatic fever
    c. Sickle cell anemia
    d. Viral infection

15. The most useful test for evaluation of suspected acute rheumatic fever is:

    a. Antistreptolysin-O (ASO) titer
    b. Electrocardiogram
    c. Hemoglobin electrophoresis
    d. Urinalysis

16. The initial attack of acute rheumatic fever is preceded by:

    a. A viral illness
    b. A group A streptococcal infection
    c. An exposure to mites
    d. An exposure to chicken pox

17. A 3-week-old infant has a 1 day history of irritability, pallor, and poor feeding. He is afebrile. On physical examination, his heart rate is 240 beats/min (bpm) while asleep. The most likely diagnosis is:

    a. Supraventricular tachycardia
    b. Premature ventricular contractions (PVCs)
    c. Sinus tachycardia
    d. Cyanotic heart defect

18. A 10-month-old infant presents with a 3-day history of fever, runny nose, and coughing. Per the parent, he has not been eating well, and only drinking a few cups of milk and juice over the last 2 days. On examination, he feels very warm, his RR is 45 and his HR is 210. He has no rashes. His abdomen is soft and round. Your initial diagnosis includes:

    a. Supraventricular tachycardia based on HR; needs immediate transfer
    b. Congestive heart failure based on HR and RR; needs immediate transfer
    c. Sinus tachycardia based on clinical history and HR; needs antipyretics and possibly fluids
    d. Kawasaki disease based on clinical history and fever; needs transfer for IV IgG

19. The most common cause of myocarditis is:

    a. Bacterial
    b. Viral
    c. Drug reaction
    d. Radiation therapy

20. Which of the following is not an expected finding in a child with myocarditis?

    a. Persistent tachycardia
    b. History of antecedent "flulike" illness
    c. A gallop rhythm
    d. A significant heart murmur

21. Which of the following is not a component of Metabolic syndrome, a clustering of factors in children shown to be associated with increased risk of coronary artery disease later in life?

    a. Obesity
    b. Elevated lipid levels
    c. Heart murmur
    d. Elevated fasting glucose level

22. Initial management of a 4-year-old, overweight boy with a repeat total cholesterol level of 185 mg/dl includes all of the following except:

    a. Educate the family about decreasing saturated fat intake to less than 7% of calories and cholesterol intake to less than 200 mg per day
    b. Blood sent for lipoprotein analysis
    c. Educate the family about decreasing/eliminating daily intake of fruit juices, sugar-sweetened food and beverages, and salt intake
    d. Educate the family about increasing aerobic activities

23. Kawasaki disease is most common in:

    a. Neonates
    b. Children younger than 5 years of age
    c. Children older than 6 years of age
    d. Females

24. A principal clinical feature that aids in the diagnosis of Kawasaki disease includes:

    a. Low-grade fever for 24 hours and a pruritic rash
    b. Conjunctivitis with exudate and facial rash
    c. Arthritis and chorea
    d. High (>39°C/102°F) fever persisting at least 5 days, and acute erythema and/or edema of hands and feet

25. An essential test in the evaluation of a 2-year-old child being managed for Kawasaki disease is:

    a. An echocardiogram
    b. Electrolytes
    c. Cholesterol
    d. Streptococcal antibody titer

◘ ANSWERS AND RATIONALE

1. **(b)** VSD is the most common defect in children either isolated or associated with other defects (9% reported or 2.5/1000 live births). The other defects are found in 0.06–0.2/1000 live births with coarctation found in 4% of CHD patients.

2. **(d)** The episode described is that of a cyanotic spell associated with tetralogy of Fallot defects. A child in congestive heart failure would be tachycardic and possibly have hepatomegaly but would not necessarily be cyanotic; an isolated acute life-threatening event (ALTE) may produce perioral cyanosis but it would not necessarily be associated with a crying episode, and the murmur lends itself to a cardiac diagnosis. Coarctation of the aorta is an acyanotic defect.

3. **(a)** Given the murmur and cyanosis, referral to a cardiology center would be appropriate. An apnea monitor would not pick up episodes of cyanosis until apnea ensues, which may be fairly delayed; keeping a diary will be helpful but should be done after being evaluated by a cardiologist. Oxygen may help temporarily but does not address the underlying etiology.

4. **(b)** While chest pain in children and adolescents is the second most common reason for referral to a cardiologist, cardiac chest pain in children is extremely rare. Chest pain in children is more typically idiopathic (21%) or related to growth and musculoskeletal issues (5%). Asthma, reflux, and psychogenic etiologies are also common. None of the other diagnoses will present with chest pain.

5. **(d)** Complete heart block in a young child will lead to a heart rate less than acceptable, which will progress to heart failure as the heart cannot meet the body's metabolic demand. Mild pulmonary stenosis would have to be very severe to cause significant obstruction that would lead to right-sided heart failure. An inflammatory heart process would have to progress to severe dysfunction to lead to heart failure. Inflammatory heart disease in infants presents with acute, severe disease that is usually fatal. Inflammatory heart disease is found frequently in the toddler-age group, typically post viral infection. β-Hemolytic group A streptococcal (GAS) pharyngitis is primarily a disease of children 5 to 15 years old and is rare in children younger than 3 years old.

6. **(d)** Both tachypnea and tachycardia are initial, general signs of congestive heart failure, hepatomegaly is a sign of right-sided failure and is found early in children. Pedal edema is less common in children than in adults. There must be a 10% increase in body weight for edema to occur, and typically the face and eyelids are noted first.

7. **(c)** A ventricular septal defect (VSD) with its left-to-right shunting will increase pulmonary blood flow and cause volume overload if large enough.

Both coarctation of the aorta and pulmonary stenosis will cause an obstructive process that may progress to CHF. SVT may progress to CHF due to decreased diastolic filling time, which leads to poor cardiac output and the elevated rate will eventually cause poor function.

8.   **(b)** A murmur from a venous hum is a continuous murmur, heard at the right upper sternal border and will disappear with position changes. A murmur associated with transposition of the great arteries will be associated with increased pulmonary blood flow (systolic murmur heard best at left upper sternal border) or an associated atrial or ventricular septal defect. It is not likely for a child to have TGA and survive to 4 years of age with no intervention. The murmur of rheumatic heart disease is associated with the mitral valve. This murmur is a systolic murmur, best heard at the left apex, extending to the left axilla.

9.   **(c)** A venous hum is due to the turbulent flow of blood draining from the head vessels into the SVC and the right atrium. When the child lies down, the flow is less turbulent and the murmur disappears. This murmur is best heard at the right upper sternal border, toward the clavicle.

10. **(d)** An innocent murmur is typically low in intensity and is only systolic. An innocent murmur is said to be heard at one time in 70–85% of all children. A holosystolic murmur and a palpable thrill are associated with pathologic murmurs. A presumed innocent murmur does not necessitate immediate cardiology referral, especially if the patient is asymptomatic. If so, the referral would be if the primary care provider wished for further confirmation of the etiology of a murmur.

11. **(c)** Based on the new 2007 guidelines, SBE prophylaxis is only recommended for children for 6 months after surgical repair and continued if they have residual defect, which would prohibit endothelialization of the surrounding tissue.

12. **(b)** Per AAP guidelines, all blood pressures should be repeated up to three times to confirm the reading. Attention must be given to accurate cuff size, anxiety regarding the procedure, and performing the blood pressure via auscultation and not with a machine for a truly accurate measurement.

13. **(b)** Coarctation of the aorta would present with hypertension in the right upper extremity. Kidney diseases such as renal artery stenosis, congenital renal abnormalities, and renal parenchymal disease are a few of the most common causes of secondary hypertension in children younger than 10 years old. Severe coronary artery disease would be rare in children and does not present with hypertension. Rheumatic fever, a VSD, and tetralogy of Fallot do not present with systemic hypertension.

14. **(b)** Symptoms such as new onset murmur associated with the mitral valve and polyarthritis of the joints particularly the knees, ankles, and elbows are two of the major criteria necessary for diagnosing rheumatic fever. Fever and arthralgia are minor criteria. While Kawasaki disease can present with high fever and joint pain, new onset murmurs are not characteristic of this disease. Sickle cell anemia alone would not present with pain and fever. A sickle cell crisis would present with painful swelling of the hands and feet as well as acute abdominal pain. The anemia would cause a notable innocent murmur but that would be a II–III/VI systolic ejection murmur typically noted at left lower sternal border or midclavicular line. Fever is not typically a presenting symptom associated with a vasoocclusive crisis. A viral illness would also not present with swollen

joints or a blowing murmur. A louder systolic ejection murmur at the lower left sternal border or midclavicular area may be noted but it would dissipate as the fever resolves.

15. **(a)** An increase in ASO titers indicates a current or recent infection with β-hemolytic group A streptococci (GAS). The other studies are not specific for rheumatic fever diagnosis.

16. **(b)** Rheumatic fever is always preceded by a β-hemolytic group A streptococcal (GAS) infection. A viral illness may precede a myocardial inflammatory process. Mites would produce localized, dermal effects. They rarely transmit disease to humans in the United States. Varicella infections have been documented as preceding myocarditis and cardiomyopathy, but this would not present with symptoms characteristic of rheumatic fever.

17. **(a)** SVT is diagnosed in this age group as a heart rate greater than 220 bpm. Sinus tachycardia is typically less than 220 bpm. PVCs would not be persistent nor would they, or a congenital heart defect, cause a heart rate to be greater than 220 bpm.

18. **(c)** As the heart rate is less than 220 bpm, this does not meet the criteria for SVT. He does not appear to be in congestive heart failure, he is mildly tachypneic explained by the fever and illness with no palpable liver.

19. **(b)** While all of these can potentially cause an inflammatory process of the heart, which may progress to myocarditis, the most common cause is typically viral, with adenovirus, Coxsackie B, cytomegalovirus, parvovirus B19, influenza, or respiratory syncytial virus being most frequently identified.

20. **(d)** Murmurs are soft, less common in myocarditis, and only noted if tricuspid or mitral insufficiency is present. The tachycardia is secondary to the inflammation and neurohormonal responses, and a preceding viral illness is very common. Often a gallop rhythm is noted because of rapid filling of a noncompliant, poorly contractile left ventricle.

21. **(c)** As heart murmurs are frequently innocent or nonpathologic in children, the presence of a heart murmur does not predict the risk of coronary artery disease later in life. All of the other issues are factors associated with Metabolic syndrome, which has been documented to predict heart disease.

22. **(a)** A repeat total fasting cholesterol level of 185 mg/dl is considered borderline. Per AAP, the American Heart Association, and the American College of Cardiology recommendations, strict dietary changes such as dropping fat and cholesterol intake are not recommended at this time. Encouraging a heart-healthy diet and aerobic activities as well as simple dietary changes that decrease refined sugars and high fat and salt intake are acceptable for all children of any age. The lipoprotein profile will provide further guidance by documenting HDL and LDL values for future monitoring.

23. **(b)** In the United States, Kawasaki disease is more common during winter and early spring months; boys outnumber girls and 76% of children are younger than 5 years of age. While Kawasaki disease may be diagnosed in the other populations, those occurrences are more atypical.

24. **(d)** The classic diagnosis of Kawasaki disease is based on the presence of a high fever for greater than or equal to 5 days along with the presence of other symptoms such as erythema of palms and soles, diffuse rash, bilateral conjunctivitis, erythema of lips, strawberry tongue, and cervical lymphadenopathy.

The rash is not typically pruritic and does not involve the face. There may be joint pain but chorea is not a classic clinical feature of Kawasaki disease.

25. **(a)** An echocardiogram is imperative for evaluation of the presence of aneurysms of the coronary arteries, LV function, and presence of pericardial effusion. The initial echocardiogram will provide a baseline for future comparisons as aneurysms may not be present within the first few days of the illness but typically present during the acute phase (first 2 weeks). Evaluating electrolytes may be helpful in management of the illness symptoms but are not diagnostic of Kawasaki disease. Streptococcal antibody titers are necessary for diagnosing rheumatic fever. Cholesterol levels have no impact on the diagnosis of Kawasaki disease.

◘ REFERENCES

American Academy of Pediatrics Committee on Nutrition. (2003). Prevention of pediatric overweight and obesity. *Pediatrics, 112*, 2, 424–430.

Dajani, A. S., Ayoub, E., Bierman, F. Z., Bisno, A. L., Denny, F. W., Durack, D. T., *et al.* (1993). Guidelines for the diagnosis of rheumatic fever: Jones criteria, updated 1992. *Circulation, 87*, 302–307.

Daniels, S. R., Greer, F. R., & the Committee on Nutrition. (2008). Lipid screening and cardiovascular health in childhood. *Pediatrics, 122*, 198–208.

Demmler, G. J. (2006). Infectious pericarditis in children. *The Pediatric Infectious Disease Journal, 25*, 2, 165–166.

Fimbres, A. M., & Shulman, S. T. (2008). Kawasaki disease. *Pediatrics in Review, 29*, 9, *308–316.*

Gerber, M. A., Baltimore, R. S., Eaton, C. B., Gewitz, M., Rowley, A. W., Shulman, S. T., *et al.* (2009). Prevention of rheumatic fever and diagnosis and treatment of acute streptococcal pharyngitis. *Circulation, 119*, 1541–1551.

Gidding, S. S., Dennison, B. A., Birch, L. L., Daniels, S. R., Gillman, M. W., Lichtenstein, A. H., *et al.* (2006). Dietary recommendations for children and adolescents: a guide for practitioners. *Pediatrics, 117*, 2, 544–559.

Kean, J. F., Lock, J. E., & Fyler, D. C. (Eds.). (2006). *Nadas' pediatric cardiology* (2nd ed.). Philadelphia, PA: Saunders-Elsevier.

May, L. E. (2008). *Pediatric heart surgery: A ready reference for professionals.* Milwaukee, WI: Maxishare.

McCrindle, B. W., Urbina, E. M., Dennison, B. A., Jacobson, M. S., Steinberger, J., Rocchini, A. P., *et al.* (2007). Drug therapy of high-risk lipid abnormalities in children and adolescents: A scientific statement from the American Heart Association Atherosclerosis, Hypertension, and Obesity in Youth Committee, Council of Cardiovascular Disease in the Young, with the Council on Cardiovascular Nursing. *Circulation, 115*, 14, 1948–1967.

National High Blood Pressure Education Program Working Group on High Blood Pressure in Children and Adolescents. (2004). The fourth report on the diagnosis, evaluation, and treatment of high blood pressure in children and adolescents. *Pediatrics, 114*, 555–576.

Newburger, J. W., Takahashi, M., Gerber, M. A., Gewitz, M. H., Tani, L. Y., Burns, J. C., *et al.* (2004). Diagnosis, treatment, and long-term management of Kawasaki disease: A statement for health professionals from the Committee on Rheumatic fever, Endocarditis, and Kawasaki disease, Council on Cardiovascular Disease in the Young, American Heart Association. *Pediatrics, 114*, 1708–1733.

O'Connor, M., McDaniel, N., & Brady, W. J. (2008). The pediatric electrocardiogram part II: Dysrhythmias. *American Journal of Emergency Medicine, 26*, 3, 348–358.

Park, N. (2007). *Pediatric cardiology for practitioners* (5th ed.). Philadelphia, PA: Mosby-Elsevier.

Pinna, G. S., Kafetzis, D. A., Tselkas, O. I., & Skevaki, C. L. (2008). Kawasaki disease: An overview. *Current Opinion in Infectious Disease, 21*, 263–270.

Schlechte, E. A., Boramanand, N., & Funk, M. (2008). Supraventricular tachycardia in the pediatric primary care setting: Age-related presentation, diagnosis, and management. *Journal of Pediatric Health Care, 22*, 5, 289–299.

Williams, C. L., Hayman, L. L., Daniels, S. R., Robinson, T. N., Steinberger, J., Pandon, S., *et al.* (2002). Cardiovascular health in childhood: A statement for health professionals from the Committee on Atherosclerosis, Hypertension, and Obesity in the Young (AHOY) of the Council on Cardiovascular Disease in the Young, American Heart Association. *Circulation, 106*, 1, 143–160.

Wilson, W., Taubert, K. A., Gewitz, M., Lockhart, P. B., Baddour, L. M., Levison, M., *et al.* (2007). Prevention of infective endocarditis: Guidelines from the American Heart Association. *Circulation, 116*, 15, 1736–1754.

5

Respiratory Disorders

Elizabeth Sloand

Select one best answer to the following questions.

1. The PNP is teaching a group of expectant parents about infant care and illness prevention. It is most important for the PNP to stress:

    a. Keeping all animals out of the house
    b. Keeping the infant away from cigarette smoke
    c. Keeping the infant well covered at night
    d. Keeping the infant away from crowds

2. Which of the following does not place an infant at increased risk for sudden infant death syndrome?

    a. Documented episodes of periodic breathing
    b. Prematurity
    c. Severe bronchopulmonary dysplasia
    d. Apnea of prematurity

3. In the management of a child with bronchiolitis, the early use of which of the following is likely to be the most beneficial?

    a. Antihistamines
    b. Broad spectrum antibiotics
    c. Fluids and nutritional support
    d. Bronchodilators

4. A NICU graduate with bronchopulmonary dysplasia (BPD) has been discharged to home. A potential problem area that requires close monitoring is:

    a. Insufficient caloric intake
    b. Atrophy of abdominal muscles due to abdominal breathing patterns
    c. Lack of tactile stimuli due to restrictions on parental handling
    d. The predisposition to development of nasal polyps

5. A 4-year-old child with cystic fibrosis (CF) comes to the primary care office with complaints of runny nose, cough, congestion, and fever. You know that children with cystic fibrosis:

    a. Are more likely to have normal CXR and LFTs findings
    b. Usually are poor eaters with accompanying poor growth
    c. Routinely take an oral mucolytic agent
    d. Warrant more liberal use of antibiotics for respiratory infections

6. To promote normal growth in the child with cystic fibrosis, dietary management should include:

   a. Limited fats and 50% more calories than usual daily allowances
   b. Liberal fats and 50% more calories than usual daily allowances
   c. The usual number of calories as indicated by height and weight plus fat soluble vitamins
   d. Limited fat and sodium in moderation

7. Mrs. S. has brought 10-day-old Jacob to the clinic because she is concerned about his breathing. She says that while she is feeding the baby, he often stops breathing for periods of about 10 seconds. History reveals that Jacob eats well, has never appeared pale or cyanotic, and has never become limp during any of the apnea episodes. Your management plan is based on which of the following?

   a. This is a normal breathing pattern for an infant.
   b. These episodes likely indicate aspiration of formula and should be evaluated.
   c. A variety of pathologic processes are associated with the episodes described.
   d. Neurologic deficits in infants are often manifested by such episodes.

Questions 8 and 9 refer to the following scenario.

Julie, age 4, has a history of asthma. Her mother brings her to the clinic and states that Julie has been coughing and wheezing severely for the past 10 hours. Physical examination reveals a respiratory rate of 14 breaths per minute. Respirations are shallow without wheezing and there are no retractions.

8. What is the most likely reason that wheezing is not auscultated?

   a. Julie is upset about something and has faked an asthma attack.
   b. Julie's mother needs education regarding identification of wheezing.
   c. Julie's condition has improved significantly.
   d. Wheezes are not being generated because breathing is shallow.

9. Appropriate initial management of Julie's condition is to:

   a. Talk with Julie alone and ask what is upsetting her
   b. Educate the mother regarding identification of wheezing
   c. Tell Julie's mother to continue with treatment that has been effective in the past
   d. Administer a bronchodilator

10. Matthew, at 5 months old, is brought to the clinic because he has been coughing and has had clear rhinorrhea for the last 2 days. His mother tells you that he has never been sick before. Family history is positive for allergies and you hear generalized wheezing. You may conclude that:

    a. Matthew has familial asthma
    b. Matthew has asthma exacerbated by a viral infection
    c. Matthew should be referred for allergy testing
    d. Asthma should not be diagnosed at this stage

11. When educating parents regarding transmission of respiratory syncytial virus (RSV), it is important to stress which of the following?

    a. Children with RSV should be totally isolated from other children.
    b. RSV can be spread by airborne droplets or from contact with a hard surface that has been contaminated.
    c. Children who attend day care centers should take prophylactic antibiotics early each fall.
    d. Wiping hard surfaces with soap and water or disinfectant will not help in the prevention of RSV transmission.

12. In mild to moderate attacks of acute asthma, albuterol should be given every 3 to 4 hours and routine medications should be:

    a. Continued as usual
    b. Discontinued until albuterol treatments are deemed unnecessary
    c. Given only if the albuterol is ineffective
    d. Be decreased to the minimum recommended dose

Questions 13 and 14 refer to the following scenario.

Josh, age 5, presents to the clinic with inspiratory stridor, drooling, and a temperature of 105°F. He insists on sitting up during the clinical examination.

13. This clinical picture is most consistent with a diagnosis of:

    a. Aspirated foreign body
    b. Reactive airway disease
    c. Viral croup
    d. Epiglottitis

14. Appropriate initial management of Josh includes:

    a. High doses of an oral broad spectrum antibiotic and antipyretics
    b. Teaching the mother to administer racemic epinephrine by nebulization
    c. Teaching the mother how to administer loading and decreasing doses of prednisone
    d. Immediate hospitalization with intravenous antibiotics

15. A diagnosis of croup is substantiated by which radiographic finding?

    a. Ground glass appearance in the upper airway
    b. Sparse areas of atelectasis
    c. "Thumb sign" on lateral view
    d. "Hourglass" narrowing in the subglottic region

16. A lethargic appearing 18-month-old child presents to the clinic with signs and symptoms of croup. Physical examination reveals a respiratory rate of 20 bpm and mild dehydration. Appropriate management includes:

    a. Instructing the mother to force fluids and use a cool mist humidifier in the child's room
    b. Instructing the mother to liberally give fluids and to encourage intake of solid food
    c. Prescribing an oral broad spectrum antibiotic and prednisone
    d. Referring the child for hospitalization and IV fluids

17. A 6-month-old boy is brought to the clinic because he has been coughing since yesterday. His mother states that he has never been sick before. She thinks he has been febrile but is not sure. Physical examination reveals a well-developed baby with a respiratory rate of 50 bpm, mild retractions, wheezes, and a dry cough. Chest radiograph reveals diffuse hyperinflation and patchy areas of infiltration. These findings are most consistent with a diagnosis of:

    a. Laryngotracheobronchitis
    b. Cystic fibrosis
    c. Bronchiolitis
    d. Respiratory distress syndrome

Questions 18 and 19 refer to the following scenario.

Brent, a 22-month-old, has been brought to the clinic by his mother who says he has been coughing for 2 days and is now making a funny noise when he breathes. Examination reveals a fussy child with a brassy cough and inspiratory stridor. Lips and nail beds are pink. Axillary temperature is 103°F and respiratory rate is 50 bpm.

18. The most likely diagnosis of Brent's condition is:

    a. Laryngotracheobronchitis
    b. Bronchiolitis
    c. Respiratory distress syndrome
    d. Reactive airway disease

19. Which diagnostic test should be ordered first for Brent?

    a. Pulmonary function tests
    b. Throat culture
    c. Radiograph of the upper airway
    d. Laryngoscopic examination

20. Emily, a 4-year-old, stays with her great aunt during the day while her mother is at work. Emily's mother has brought her to the clinic because the great aunt has just been diagnosed with TB. Emily's Mantoux skin test is positive but there is no clinical or radiographic evidence of disease. Appropriate management includes:

    a. Reassuring Emily's mother that no treatment is needed
    b. Administering another skin test in 3 months
    c. Oral penicillin therapy
    d. Oral preventive isoniazid therapy

Questions 21, 22, and 23 refer to the following scenario.

The mother of 2-year-old Heather has brought her to the clinic with a "bad cough." History reveals onset of illness four days ago with clear rhinorrhea and coughing.

Her mother says that Heather's fever has been as high as 103°F under the arm. Physical examination reveals a temperature of 101°F (axillary) and respiratory rate of 56 bpm, with slight nasal flaring and intercostal, subcostal, and suprasternal retractions. The pharynx is red without tonsillar exudate. Chest auscultation reveals widespread rales and wheezing. The lips and nail beds are slightly pale but pink, skin turgor is good, and mucous membranes are moist.

21. The most likely diagnosis of Heather's condition is:

    a. Viral pneumonia
    b. Pneumococcal pneumonia
    c. Streptococcal pneumonia
    d. *Haemophilus influenzae* type b pneumonia

22. Initially, Heather should receive which diagnostic test?

    a. Sputum culture
    b. Sputum gram stain
    c. Chest radiograph
    d. Erythrocyte sedimentation rate

23. When deciding whether Heather should be treated at home or in the hospital, it is most important to consider Heather's:

    a. Maximum temperature
    b. Frequency of coughing episodes
    c. Hydration status
    d. Total length of illness

◘ ANSWERS AND RATIONALE

1. **(b)** Exposure to cigarette smoke has been associated with increased incidence of illnesses such as asthma, bronchiolitis, and otitis media in children. None of the other options is as strongly associated with childhood illness

2. **(a)** Infantile apnea or periodic breathing (periods of less than 15 to 20 seconds) without pallor, cyanosis, or limpness is normal and is not related to SIDS. Other answers have been associated with increased incidence of SIDS

3. **(c)** Medications are not routinely recommended. Bronchodilators and corticosteroids can be used in select infants. Antibiotics are indicated if bacterial infection is suspected.

4. **(a)** The pathophysiology of BPD is similar to chronic obstructive lung disease (COLD). Diuretic use and limitation of fluids is often part of the

management plan. Limitation of fluids may make it difficult to provide adequate caloric intake

5. **(d)** Children with CF are more vulnerable to serious respiratory infection, so liberal use of antibiotics is the best course of action.

6. **(b)** Because of steatorrhea and metabolic demands, the child with cystic fibrosis should receive 50% more calories than the usual daily allowance. Liberal fat should be allowed in the diet and may even be supplemented with MCT oil and Polycose.

7. **(a)** Brief apnea episodes (less than 15 to 20 seconds) are normal in infants and are most frequent in preterm infants. These normal episodes are not associated with pallor, cyanosis, or hypotonia.

8. **(d)** A respiratory rate of 14 breaths per minute is slow for a 4-year-old child and is an indicator that there is muscle fatigue or that the child is in extreme respiratory distress. When the wheezing child develops muscle fatigue, a wheeze may not be generated, even in the presence of severe obstruction.

9. **(d)** When there are signs of muscle fatigue, and breathing is shallow in a known asthmatic, a bronchodilator should be given to help relieve airway obstruction.

10. **(d)** Asthma is not diagnosed during a child's first episode of wheezing but after a documented pattern of recurrent wheezing responsive to bronchodilator therapy. Differential diagnoses should include foreign body, congenital malformation, and bronchiolitis.

11. **(b)** The virus can be spread both directly and indirectly. One means of RSV transmission is by touching an RSV contaminated fomite, such as a counter, doorknob, or crib rail. Cleaning such environmental surfaces can be effective, as RSV can live for many hours on such surfaces.

12. **(a)** Routine asthma medications should continue even when albuterol is needed. A review of routine medications may indicate a step up in controller medicines.

13. **(d)** Epiglottitis usually occurs in children ages 2 to 6 years, while croup usually occurs in children ages 3 months to 3 years. The child with epiglottitis runs a high fever, drools, and insists on sitting up, usually leaning forward in the "tripod" position.

14. **(d)** Epiglottitis progresses quickly and is a medical emergency. Initial therapy is hospitalization.

15. **(d)** Inflammation in the subglottic region causes narrowing, resulting in an "hourglass" or "steeple" sign seen best on posteroanterior view.

16. **(d)** A respiratory rate of 20 bpm in an 18-month-old child, accompanied by lethargy and mild dehydration, likely indicates that the child has become fatigued from the increased effort of breathing. The child should be hospitalized and given IV fluids to allow for rest and rehydration while respiratory status is closely monitored.

17. **(c)** The infant with bronchiolitis typically presents with low-grade fever, cough, dyspnea, and wheezing. Chest radiograph reveals hyperinflation and perhaps patchy infiltrates. Laryngotracheobronchitis produces a barking cough without the stated radiograph findings. History of frequent illness is common with cystic fibrosis. Respiratory distress syndrome is a disease of the newborn.

18. **(a)** Laryngotracheobronchitis (croup) is the most common cause of stridor. Stridor is usually caused by an upper-airway condition. Other answers are not upper-airway conditions.

19. **(c)** Since stridor is usually caused by an upper-airway condition such as croup, epiglottitis, or foreign body aspiration, radiograph of the upper airway is helpful in diagnosing the cause of stridor. Laryngoscopic examination is an invasive and dangerous procedure, and would not be used for initial diagnostic purposes.

20. **(d)** Isoniazid therapy is indicated if a child has a positive TB skin test and known exposure to TB even if there is no clinical or radiographic evidence of disease. Referral to a pediatric pulmonary specialist and reporting to the health department are also indicated.

21. **(a)** Respiratory viruses (particularly RSV, adenoviruses, parainfluenza virus types 1, 2, and 3), and enterovirus are the most common cause of pneumonia during the first several years of life. The condition is usually preceded by rhinitis and cough for several days. Temperatures with viral pneumonia are generally lower than with bacterial pneumonia. Rales and wheezing are common.

22. **(c)** Pneumonia is diagnosed by chest radiograph. Other tests listed can indicate infection or inflammation, but not pneumonia.

23. **(c)** Children with viral pneumonia are usually treated at home with supportive measures unless they need intravenous fluids, oxygen, or assisted ventilation.

◻ REFERENCES

American Academy of Pediatrics. (2002). Clinical Practice Guideline: Diagnosis and Management of Childhood Obstructive Sleep Apnea Syndrome. *Pediatrics, 109,* 704–712.

American Academy of Pediatrics. (2009). *Red book: 2009 Report of the committee on infectious diseases* (28th ed.). Elk Grove Village, IL: American Academy of Pediatrics.

Au, C. T., & Li, A. M. (2009). Obstructive Sleep Breathing Disorders. *Pediatric Clinics of North America, 56,* 1, 243–259.

Berkowitz C. D. (2004). SIDS (Sudden Infant Death Syndrome) and ALTE (Apparent Life-Threatening Event). In J. E. Tintinalli, G. D. Kelen, J. S. Stapczynski, O. J. Ma, & D. M. Cline (Eds.), *Emergency Medicine: A Comprehensive Study Guide* (6th ed.). Available at: http://www.accessemergencymedicine.com/ontent.aspx?aID=596030. Accessed June 28, 2009.

Bhandari A., & Bhandari V. (2009). Pitfalls, problems, and progress in bronchopulmonary dysplasia. *Pediatrics, 123,* 6, 1562–1573.

Committee on Fetus and Newborn. (2003). American Academy of Pediatrics Policy Statement: Apnea, sudden infant death syndrome, and home monitoring. *Pediatrics, 111,* 4, 914–917.

Burns, C. E., Dunn, A. M., Brady, M. A., Starr, N. B., & Blosser, C. G. (Eds.). (2008). *Pediatric primary care* (4th ed.). St. Louis, MO: Elsevier Saunders.

DeWolfe, C. C. (2005). Apparent life-threatening event: A review. *Pediatric Clinics of North America, 52,* 4, 1127–1146.

Hay, W., Levin, M., Sondheimer, J., Deterding, R. (2009). *Current diagnosis and treatment pediatrics.* New York, NY: McGraw-Hill.

Kliegman, R. M., Behman, R., Jenson, H. B., & Stanton, B. (Eds.). (2007). *Nelson textbook of pediatrics* (18th ed.). Philadelphia, PA: W. B. Saunders.

McGovern M. C., & Smith, M. B. H. (2004). Causes of apparent life threatening events in infants: A systematic review. *Archives of Disease in Childhood, 89,* 11, 1043–1048.

Meissner, H. C., Long, S. S., & Committee on Infectious Diseases, and Committee on Fetus and Newborn. (2003). Revised Indications for the Use of Palivizumab and Respiratory Syncytial Virus Immune Globulin Intravenous for the Prevention of Respiratory Syncytial Virus Infections. *Pediatrics, 112,* 6, 1447–1452.

National Heart, Lung, and Blood Institute. (2007). *Expert panel report 3: Guidelines for the diagnosis and management of asthma.* Available at: http://www.nhlbi.nih.gov/guidelines/asthma/asthgdln.pdf. Accessed June 27, 2009.

O'Sullivan, B. P., & Freedman, S. D. (2009). Cystic fibrosis. *The Lancet, 373,* 1891–1904.

Powell, D. A., & Hunt, W. G. (2006). Tuberculosis in children: An update. *Advances in Pediatrics, 53,* 279–322.

Proesmans, M., Vermeulen, F., & Boeck, K. (2008). What's new in cystic fibrosis? From treating symptoms to correction of the basic defect. *European Journal of Pediatrics, 167,* 839–849.

Ratcliffe, M. M., & Kieckhefer, G. M. (2009). Asthma. In P. Jackson Allen, J. A. Vessey, & N. Schapiro (Eds.), *Primary care of the child with a chronic condition* (5th ed., pp. 168–196). St. Louis, MO: Mosby.

Schechter, M. S., & Section on Pediatric Pulmonary Subcommittee on Obstructive Sleep Apnea Syndrome. (2002). Technical report: Diagnosis and management of childhood obstructive sleep apnea syndrome. *Pediatrics, 109,* 4, e69.

Shah, S., & Sharieff, G. Q. (2007). Pediatric respiratory infections. *Emergency Medicine Clinics of North America, 25,* 4, 961–979.

Taussig, L. M., & Landau, L. I. (Eds.) (2008). *Pediatric emergency medicine* (2nd ed.). Philadelphia, PA: Mosby Elsevier.

Taylor, Z., Nolan, C. M., & Blumberg, H. M. (2005). Controlling tuberculosis in the United States: Recommendations from the American Thoracic Society, CDC, and the Infectious Diseases Society of America. *Morbidity and Mortality Weekly Report, 54,* RR12, 1–81.

Tippets, B., & Guilbert, T. (2009). Managing asthma in children, part 1: Making the diagnosis and assessing severity. *Consultant for Pediatricians, 8,* 5, 168–174.

Tippets, B., & Guilbert, T. (2009). Managing asthma in children, part 2: Achieving and maintaining control. *Consultant for Pediatricians, 8,* 6, 221–227.

6

Dermatologic Disorders

Jeanne Steman Findlay

Select one best answer to the following questions.

1. A 7-year-old African American female presents with several hyperkeratotic raised, periungual lesions on the two middle fingers of her left hand. She has a history of nail biting. The most likely diagnosis is:

   a. Impetigo
   b. Molluscum contagiosum
   c. Verruca vulgaris
   d. Herpetic whitlow

2. Which of the following secondary skin changes is not associated with atopic dermatitis?

   a. Lichenification
   b. Striae
   c. Pigment changes
   d. Excoriations

3. In infants, the lesions associated with atopic dermatitis are most likely to be distributed on the:

   a. Cheeks and forehead
   b. Wrists and ankles
   c. Antecubital and popliteal fossae
   d. Flexural surfaces

4. During your newborn examination of K. L., you note a generalized lacy reticulated blue discoloration. This clinical presentation describes:

   a. Harlequin color change
   b. Mongolian spots
   c. Blue nevus
   d. Cutis marmorata

5. During 3-year-old J. T.'s physical examination, you observe eight, light brown macules, ranging in size from 0.5 to 0.75 cm on his trunk, arms, and legs. Your management plan would be to:

   a. Educate the family to apply sunscreen frequently
   b. Explain that the lesions will fade with time
   c. Refer to a dermatologist
   d. Document the findings and reevaluate in six months

6. Mrs. Franklin is concerned about a light pink lesion on the back of 2-month-old Aaron's neck that darkens with crying. This description is consistent with:

   a. Sturge-Weber disease
   b. Salmon patch
   c. Port-wine stain
   d. Hemangioma

7. D. M., 7 years old, presents with a beefy red macular–papular rash in the diaper area with satellite lesions on the abdomen. The appropriate treatment would be:

    a. Clotrimazole
    b. A & D ointment
    c. Gentian violet 1 to 2%
    d. Cornstarch

Questions 8 and 9 refer to the following scenario.

The mother of 4-month-old T. W. states that the infant has been irritable and has not been sleeping well. During the physical examination, you note papular lesions on his feet and erythematous papules over his back.

8. To confirm your suspicion of scabies you would order a:

    a. Wood's lamp examination
    b. Microscopic skin scraping
    c. KOH preparation of skin scraping
    d. Skin culture

9. Having confirmed the diagnosis of scabies in T. W., the treatment of choice would be:

    a. Permethrin 5%
    b. Lindane 1%
    c. Sulfur ointment 6%
    d. Crotamiton 10%

10. Which of the following statements regarding treatment of pediculosis capitis is true?

    a. Carpeting and furniture must be shampooed and sprayed with a pediculicide.
    b. Nonwashable items that have come into contact with an infected person should be sealed in plastic bags for 2 to 4 weeks.
    c. Hair must be trimmed close to the scalp to insure elimination of nits.
    d. Frequent shampooing with Permethrin 1% will prevent reinfestation.

11. You note a single, large, oval, pink patch with central clearing on 16-year-old M. P.'s back. Lesions are not present elsewhere. Results of a KOH preparation of the lesion are negative. This would confirm a diagnosis of:

    a. Seborrheic dermatitis
    b. Secondary syphilis
    c. Tinea corporis
    d. Pityriasis rosea

12. Mrs. J. brings her 6-year-old son in because of "hives" that she describes as a red raised rash. Which finding below would support a diagnosis of erythema multiforme rather than urticaria?

    a. Lesions that blanch with pressure
    b. Eyelid edema
    c. Lesions that are present for more than 24 hours
    d. Intense pruritus

13. When examining 7-month-old R.V., you note red scaly plaques in his diaper area, particularly in the inguinal folds, with satellite lesions on his abdomen. The appropriate treatment would be:

    a. Petrolatum/lanolin ointment
    b. Petroleum jelly
    c. Zinc oxide
    d. Nystatin

Questions 14, 15, and 16 refer to the following scenario.

During 15-year-old N. M.'s routine physical examination, she complains of getting pimples all the time. You note open and closed comedones over her forehead and chin. There are more than 15 papules and pustules, but no cysts.

14. N. M.'s clinical presentation is consistent with:

    a. Comedonal acne
    b. Mild acne
    c. Moderate acne
    d. Severe acne

15. Which of the medications below is the appropriate choice?

    a. Antiandrogens
    b. Isotretinoin
    c. Minocycline
    d. Corticosteroids

16. Which of the following statements is not consistent with an appropriate management plan for acne?

    a. Improvement with use of kerato-lytic agents should occur within 4 to 6 weeks.
    b. Facial scrubs are recommended before applying topical antibiotics.
    c. Noncomedogenic moisturizers and cosmetics may be used.
    d. Sunscreens should always be used in conjunction with retinoic acid.

17. H. B. is 2 days old. Her mother calls and reports a rash consisting of redness with yellow-white "bumps" all over her body except for the palms and soles. The infant most likely has:

    a. Erythema toxicum
    b. Transient neonatal pustular melanosis
    c. Molluscum contagiosum
    d. Milia

Questions 18 and 19 refer to the following scenario.

L. R., at 6 years of age, presents at clinic with a solitary nonpruritic lesion around his upper lip. Closer inspection reveals some vesicles and honey-colored crusts.

18. The most likely diagnosis is:

    a. Herpes simplex
    b. Varicella
    c. Nummular eczema
    d. Impetigo

19. The treatment of choice for L. R. would be:

    a. Acyclovir
    b. Topical steroids
    c. Topical antibiotics
    d. Petrolatum/lanolin ointment

20. D. J. is a 4-year-old African American child with a depigmented macular on his forehead. The lesion has sharp borders. No scales are present. The most appropriate treatment would be:

    a. 1% hydrocortisone
    b. Alpha hydroxy acid
    c. Ketoconazole
    d. Silver sulfadiazine

21. While examining 7-year-old S. R.'s scalp you note three small patches of hair loss. Broken hair is present, as is erythema and scaling. Based on this information, which of the following diagnoses is most likely?

    a. Tinea capitis
    b. Traction alopecia
    c. Trichotillomania
    d. Alopecia areata

◘ ANSWERS AND RATIONALE

1. **(c)** Common warts are found most usually on fingers, hands, and feet in children and are often preceded by trauma such as nail biting or picking at cuticles.

2. **(b)** Striae describes skin that has been stretched, whereas the skin in atopic dermatitis is thickened, crusted, and hyperpigmented.

3. **(a)** The infantile phase of atopic dermatitis follows a different distribution pattern than that associated with the childhood phase, which may include the face, trunk, and extensor surfaces.

4. **(d)** Mongolian spots and blue nevus have a bluish discoloration. Cutis marmorata is the only condition that is generalized. Harlequin color change is more red than pale.

5. **(c)** The lesions described are café au lait spots. Six or more of these lesions may indicate neurofibromatosis and should be referred for further evaluation.

6. **(b)** A salmon patch is a flat, light pink to light red mark seen on the eyelid, glabella, or nape of neck that intensifies with crying.

7. **(a)** The rash described is *Candida albicans* and should be treated with an antifungal agent.

8. **(b)** Microscopic skin scrapings of burrows will reveal the mite, eggs, or feces if scabies are present. Although skin scrapings are not routinely done, they are definitive if there is any doubt of the diagnosis.

9. **(a)** Permethrin is the only safe choice in this case. Lindane is contraindicated in infants younger than 6 months of age. Sulfur ointment and crotamiton are not as effective and are difficult to use.

10. **(b)** Objects that cannot be washed should be sealed in plastic bags. Since eggs mature in 7 to 10 days, 2 to 4 weeks should be sufficient to prevent reinfestation. Frequent shampooing and close haircuts are unnecessary and may contribute to a feeling of shame and embarrassment. Environmental cleaning includes vacuuming, although sprays are not recommended.

11. **(d)** Pityriasis rosea presents with a herald patch, is probably viral, and thus will not reveal hyphae or spores seen in the KOH scrapings of fungal infections such as tinea. The location of the patch and its absence on the mucosa, palms, and soles distinguish it from seborrheic dermatitis and secondary syphilis.

12. **(c)** Urticarial lesions tend to be pruritic and blanch with pressure but generally fade within a few hours. Due to the large number of mast cells present in the eyelids, edema is common with urticaria. The lesions of erythema multiforme are fixed and present for up to 2 to 3 weeks.

13. **(d)** Options "a," "b," and "c" are all ointments, which act as barriers to irritants such as urine and feces. The presence of satellite lesions indicate a candida rash requiring an antifungal such as nystatin.

14. **(c)** Mild acne is characterized by open and closed comedones and occasional pustules, whereas comedonal acne is limited to open and closed comedones only. Moderate acne is characterized by open and closed comedones, papules, and pustules. Severe acne, in addition to the lesions described above, also involves cysts.

15. **(c)** Moderate acne includes open and closed comedones, papules, and pustules. Oral antibiotics are used to control moderate papulopustular acne in addition to topical keratolytics. Antiandrogens are not recommended. Corticosteroids may be used for more severe forms or the flare-ups associated with isotretinoin therapy.

16. **(b)** Facial scrubs are not recommended, and may exacerbate acne.

17. **(a)** The location (all over the body) and type of lesion (papule as opposed to vesicle) are consistent with the rash seen in erythema toxicum.

18. **(d)** The classic presentation of impetigo is that of vesicles that rupture leaving honey-colored crusts.

19. **(c)** Impetigo is a bacterial infection, most likely caused by *Staphylococcus aureus*, group A β-hemolytic streptococcus, or *Streptococcus pyogenes*. Mild cases may be treated with topical antibiotics; if no resolution, systemic antibiotics may be necessary.

20. **(a)** The most likely diagnosis is vitiligo, an area of depigmented skin more common in African Americans. It responds to steroids 30 to 50% of the time. Antifungals, antibiotics, or keratolytics would be of no value.

21. **(a)** Erythema, scaling, and broken hair are characteristic findings associated with tinea capitis. Traction alopecia may have associated erythema but not scaling. While neither trichotillomania or alopecia areata are associated with erythema or scaling, only alopecia areata is noted for total hair loss.

◼ REFERENCES

American Academy of Pediatrics. (2009). *Red book: 2009 report of the committee on infectious diseases* (28th ed.). Elk Grove Village, IL: American Academy of Pediatrics.

Burns, C. E., Dunn, A. M., Brady, M. A., Starr, N. B., & Blosser, C. (2008). *Pediatric primary care: A handbook for nurse practitioners*. Philadelphia, PA: W. B. Saunders.

Cohen, B. A. (2005). *Pediatric dermatology* (3rd ed.). Philadelphia, PA: Mosby Yearbook.

Cohen, B. A., & Lehmann, C. U. (2009). DermAtlas. Available at: http://www.dermatlas .com/derm/. Accessed January 16, 2010.

Crowson, A. N., Magro, C. M., & Mihm, M. C. (2001). *The melanocytic proliferation: A comprehensive textbook of pigmented lesions*. New York, NY: John Wiley & Sons.

Fitzpatrick, T., Johnson, R. A., Wolff, K., & Suurmond, D. (2009). *Color atlas and synopsis of clinical dermatology* (6th ed.). St. Louis, MO: McGraw-Hill.

Hay, W., Levin, M., Deterding, R., & Sondheimer, J. (2009). *Current diagnosis and treatment: Pediatric* (19th ed.). New York, NY: Lange Medical Books/McGraw-Hill.

Morrell, D. S., & Burkhart, D. N. (2009). Dermatologic therapies, part I. *Pediatric Annals, 38*, 6, 300.

Morrell, D. S., & Burkhart, D. N. (2009). Dermatologic therapies, part II. *Pediatric Annals, 38*, 7, 368–395.

Pomerantz, A. J., & O'Brien, T. (2007). *Nelson's instructions for pediatric patients*. St. Louis, MO: Elsevier.

7

Gastrointestinal Disorders

Lindsay Wilson

Select one best answer to the following questions.

Questions 1 and 2 refer to the following scenario.

The mother of 4-month-old N. D. reports episodes of vomiting and diarrhea beginning 2 days ago. He has also had several episodes of screaming and drawing up his legs. Prior to this he has been healthy with a normal weight gain.

1. The least likely diagnosis is:

    a. Incarcerated hernia
    b. Gastroenteritis
    c. Intussusception
    d. Pyloric stenosis

2. Physical examination of N. D. reveals a sausage-shaped mass and guaiac-positive stool. This would confirm a diagnosis of:

    a. Incarcerated hernia
    b. Gastroenteritis
    c. Intussusception
    d. Pyloric stenosis

3. R. D., at 14 years of age, presents with a complaint of abdominal pain that has occurred several times over the past 3 months. She describes the pain as an intermittent sharp pain, occasionally relieved with a heating pad. Her physical examination is within normal limits. You suspect recurrent abdominal pain (RAP). Which clinical finding is most consistent with RAP?

    a. Periumbilical pain
    b. Constipation
    c. Pain worsens with defecation
    d. Weight loss

4. Education and counseling of the parents of a 4-month-old child with gastroesophageal reflux should include all of the following except?

    a. Thicken formula with rice cereal
    b. Change to a hypoallergenic formula
    c. Place infant in car seat after feeding
    d. Avoid exposure of the infant to tobacco smoke

5. B. W., at 6 years of age, complains of sharp epigastric pain radiating to his back. Which laboratory data would be consistent with these physical signs?

   a. Decreased serum albumin
   b. Elevated serum amylase
   c. Elevated serum gastrin
   d. Decreased serum protein

6. An umbilical hernia:

   a. Occurs more frequently in full-term infants
   b. Resolves spontaneously in 3 to 6 months
   c. Is frequently associated with diastasis recti
   d. Responds well to taping

7. S. L., at 9 years of age, is brought to the clinic for evaluation of abdominal pain that wakes her at night. Her parents have recently divorced and she is attending a new school. She has missed 8 days of school in the past 6 weeks. She reports occasional emesis. An appropriate management plan would be:

   a. A bland diet with small frequent feedings
   b. A referral to a gastroenterologist
   c. To stress importance of school attendance
   d. To consult with the school psychologist

Questions 8 and 9 refer to the following scenario.

J. D., at 7 months of age, is seen with a 2-day history of diarrhea. He has had three to four wet diapers in the past 24 hours. The anterior fontanel is slightly depressed. Capillary refill is normal.

8. Which degree of dehydration is most consistent with these findings?

   a. 1 to 2%
   b. 3 to 5%
   c. 6 to 10%
   d. Greater than 10%

9. Based on your assessment of J. D., the appropriate management plan for his dehydration would be to:

   a. Begin BRAT diet
   b. Withhold formula for 24 hours and give electrolyte solution
   c. Begin rehydration in the office and observe for 3 to 4 hours
   d. Refer immediately for parenteral fluids

10. A. W., at 3 days old, presents with vomiting, abdominal distention, and constipation. Which of the following should be included in the differential diagnosis?

    a. Hirschsprung disease
    b. Pyloric stenosis
    c. Celiac disease
    d. Meckel diverticulum

11. C. R., 4 years old, was diagnosed with celiac disease at age 18 months. In addition to closely monitoring her growth, you also monitor for anemia. At this visit her laboratory results confirm an elevated MCV. An appropriate follow-up laboratory test would be serum:

    a. Protein
    b. Ferritin
    c. Folate
    d. Transferrin

12. Justin, 11 years old, presents with complaints of chronic diarrhea and abdominal pain. You note a 5-kg weight loss from last year's annual examination. Today, his examination reveals right lower quadrant pain and perianal skin tags. The most likely diagnosis is:

    a. Encopresis
    b. Crohn's disease
    c. Irritable bowel disease
    d. Ulcerative colitis

Questions 13 and 14 refer to the following scenario.

E. G., at 9 years of age, presents with diffuse abdominal pain and acute onset of diarrhea described as a frequent urge to defecate. She is passing large amounts of flatus, small amounts of stool, and complains of tenderness during rectal examination.

13. This clinical picture is highly suggestive of:

    a. Gastroenteritis
    b. Ulcerative colitis
    c. Giardiasis
    d. Appendicitis

14. Which of the following laboratory tests would confirm your diagnosis for E. G.?

    a. Serum albumin
    b. Abdominal ultrasound
    c. Stool for ova and parasites
    d. Bone age

15. Sam, at 8 years of age, presents to your clinic with his third episode of diarrhea in 3 months. He also complains of frequent flatulence and a decreased appetite. After going over the history, you recall that he went on a camping trip with his Cub Scout troop several months ago. What is his most likely diagnosis?

    a. Celiac disease
    b. Giardiasis
    c. Rotovirus
    d. Crohn's disease

16. J. V., 7 years old, presents with a 1-week history of fever, nausea, and anorexia. His mother reports that his skin "looks funny" as well. Further laboratory studies confirm a diagnosis of viral hepatitis. Which type of hepatitis is the most likely?

    a. Hepatitis A
    b. Hepatitis B
    c. Hepatitis C
    d. Hepatitis D

17. C. A., who is 2 weeks old, is being seen for the first time since discharge from the newborn nursery. She currently weighs 3.6 kg, which is 0.3 kg below her birth weight. While interviewing her mother you learn she has been using too little water when preparing the formula. Which of the following symptoms is least likely related to this error?

    a. Vomiting
    b. Diarrhea
    c. Dehydration
    d. Flatus

18. Vomitus that is bilious suggests:

    a. GI obstruction proximal to the pylorus
    b. GI obstruction below the ampulla of Vater
    c. Pyloric stenosis
    d. Peptic ulcer disease

19. J. P., at 5 years of age, presents with a history of stool staining his underwear, evidence of bright red blood after wiping, and abdominal discomfort. The physical examination reveals moderate abdominal distension with a midline abdominal mass. Rectal examination is positive for an impacted rectum and two small anal fissures. The priority in your management plan would be:

    a. Increasing water and fiber in the diet, and limiting milk intake
    b. Regular toilet sitting for 10 minutes, 3 times per day
    c. Two fleet enemas
    d. Mineral oil after breakfast and before bed

20. Which of the following would not be included in the management of pinworms?

    a. Nutritional support and iron supplementation
    b. Simultaneous treatment of all family members
    c. Washing bed linen in hot water
    d. Keeping fingernails short and clean

21. Mrs. D. reports starting her 6-month-old infant on rice cereal sweetened with one tablespoon of honey. In addition, the infant is consuming 42 oz. of formula. His height and weight are at 50% on the growth curve. You would recommend:

    a. Adding pureed vegetables
    b. Substituting 4-oz. juice for a formula feeding
    c. Adding scrambled egg whites
    d. Discontinuing honey

◘ ANSWERS AND RATIONALE

1. **(d)** Pyloric stenosis occurs during the first few weeks of life with projectile vomiting and weight loss.

2. **(c)** Invagination of the bowel can result in a sausagelike mass being palpated in the upper right quadrant of the abdomen with occasional bloody stools.

3. **(a)** Recurrent abdominal pain is almost always nonorganic in origin. Other than complaints of pain, usually peri-umbilical or midepigastric, the history and physical examination are normal.

4. **(c)** Sitting the infant in a car seat or other similar device compresses the stomach, making the infant more likely to reflux. A 2-week trial of a hypoallergenic formula is suggested as reflux may be due to milk protein allergy. Secondhand smoke exacerbates reflux. Thickening the formula with rice cereal reduces regurgitation and improves quality of life for the caregivers.

5. **(b)** The physical signs described are characteristic of pancreatitis, which can be confirmed with a serum amylase. Decreased serum albumin and protein are associated with Crohn's disease. The clinical picture of Crohn's disease usually includes cramping and does not radiate to the back.

6. **(c)** Umbilical hernias are a result of incomplete closure of the fascia of the umbilical ring, which, if small, may close in 1 year. The incidence is higher in low birth weight and premature infants. There is no evidence that manual reduction such as taping hastens closure.

7. **(b)** Initially because of the social history, one might think that this recurrent abdominal pain is part of school refusal syndrome. However, the night waking and occasional emesis suggests peptic ulcer disease. Changes in diet are not usually effective in treating peptic ulcers. This warrants immediate referral to a gastroenterologist.

8. **(c)** A depressed fontanel and decreased urinary output are indicative of moderate (8%) dehydration.

9. **(c)** The appropriate treatment for moderate dehydration is oral rehydration begun at the healthcare setting and observation until the rehydration phase is completed.

10. **(a)** Age and clinical findings are helpful in establishing this diagnosis. Celiac disease presents with diarrhea. Pyloric stenosis is not associated with abdominal distention, and Meckel diverticulum presents in the toddler period as painless rectal bleeding. Hirschsprung should be suspected in any newborn with abdominal distention and difficulty passing stool.

11. **(c)** Celiac disease is frequently associated with folic acid deficiency. An elevated MCV indicates macrocytosis. Anemia due to folate deficiency is macrocytic.

12. **(b)** While abdominal pain and diarrhea are common to all the choices, the right lower quadrant pain is more suggestive of Crohn's disease. Perianal skin tags are common in Crohn's disease but would be unlikely in the others.

13. **(d)** Large amounts of gas and watery stools occur about 15% of the time in appendicitis, and pain upon rectal examination is a classic symptom.

14. **(b)** Abdominal ultrasound can reveal an enlarged appendix and help to eliminate ovarian or pelvic disease. Serum albumin and ESR would be useful in diagnosing ulcerative colitis. Stool for O & P would be diagnostic of giardiasis.

15. **(b)** Giardiasis is the most common intestinal protozoal infection in children in the United States. Infection is acquired through the fecal–oral route and is associated with contaminated drinking water, especially in rural areas. It causes chronic, intermittent diarrhea, flatulence, poor appetite, and weight loss. There is no fever or blood in the stool.

16. **(a)** The acute onset and presence of fever as well as jaundice is associated with hepatitis A. Fevers are less common with the other viral hepatitis conditions.

17. **(d)** Vomiting in the newborn period may be caused by improper preparation of formula. Too little water will increase the GI and renal solute load, which may result in vomiting, diarrhea, and dehydration. Flatus is usually a result of swallowing too much air.

18. **(b)** Vomiting bile is generally considered a serious sign that usually indicates an obstruction below the ampulla of Vater.

19. **(c)** The clinical picture is consistent with encopresis. The abdomen can be distended and often a mass is palpated. Anal fissures may be present from straining, but skin tags are unlikely. The first step in treatment is to remove the impaction. Once the colon is cleared, maintenance with stool softeners, diet, and regular toileting is appropriate.

20. **(a)** Pinworms are a common parasite infecting children. They are easily treated with medication and simple environmental measures. No nutritional deficiencies are associated with pinworms.

21. **(d)** Honey may contain *Clostridium botulinum* spores and should not be given to infants younger than 1 year old. Adding vegetables is appropriate, but the risk of infant botulism is potentially life threatening. Although juice may be added, it should not be substituted for formula. Egg whites may be added at the end of the first year.

◘ REFERENCES

American Academy of Pediatrics. (2006). *Red book: 2006 report of the committee on infectious diseases* (28th ed.). Elk Grove Village, IL: American Academy of Pediatrics.

American Academy of Pediatrics. (2009). *Red book online.* Available at: http://aapredbook.aappublications.org/. Accessed January 16, 2010.

Baker, S. S., Liptak, G. S., Colletti, R. B., Croffie, J. M., DiLorenzo, C., Ector, W., *et al.* (2006). Evaluation and treatment of constipation in infants and children: Recommendations of the North American Society for Pediatric Gastroenterology, Hepatology and Nutrition. *Journal of Pediatric Gastroenterology and Nutrition, 43,* 3, e1–e13.

Carroll, A. E., Garrison, M. M., & Christakis, P. H. (2002). A systematic review of nonpharmacological and nonsurgical therapies for gastroesophageal reflux in infants. *Archives of Pediatric and Adolescent Medicine, 156,* 2, 109–113.

DiLorenzo, C., Colletti, R. B., Lehmann, H. P., Boyle, J. T., Gerson, W. T., Hyams, J. S., *et al.* (2005). Technical report: Chronic abdominal pain in children. *Journal of Pediatric Gastroenterology and Nutrition, 40,* 3, 249–261.

Garcia-Peña, B. M., Taylor, G. A., Fishman, S. J., & Mandi, K. D. (2000). Costs and effectiveness of ultrasonography and limited computed tomography for diagnosing appendicitis in children. *Pediatrics, 106,* 4, 672–676.

Maheshwai, N. (2007). Are young infants treated with erythromycin at risk for developing hypertrophic pyloric stenosis? *Archives of Diseases of Childhood, 92,* 271–273.

McCollough, M., & Sharieff, G. Q. (2003). Abdominal surgical emergencies in infants in young children. *Emergency Medical Clinics of North America, 21,* 4, 909–935.

Naik-Mathuria, B., & Olutoye, O. (2006). Foregut abnormalities. *Surgical Clinics of North America, 86,* 2, 261–284.

Rudolph, C. D., Mazur, L. J., Liptak, G. S., Baker, R. D., Boyle, J. T., Colletti, R. B., *et al.* (2001). Pediatric gastroesophageal reflux clinical practice guidelines: Guidelines for evaluation and treatment of gastroesophageal reflux in infants and children. *Journal of Pediatric Gastroenterology & Nutrition, 32,* Suppl. 2, S1–S31.

Scholl, J., & Allen, P. J. (2007). A primary care approach to functional abdominal pain. *Pediatric Nursing, 33,* 3, 247–259.

Sondheimer, J. (2003). Gastrointestinal tract. In W. W. Hay, Jr., M. J. Levin, J. M. Sondheimer, & R. R. Deterding (Eds.). *Current Pediatric Diagnosis and Treatment* (pp. 614–643). New York, NY: Lange Medical Books/McGraw-Hill.

Vandenplas, Y., Rudolph, C. D., DiLorenzo, C., Hassall, E., Uptak, G., Mazur, L., *et al.* (2009). Pediatric gastroesophageal reflux clinical practice guidelines: Joint recommendations of the North American Society for Pediatric Gastroenterology, Hepatology, and Nutrition (NASPGHAN) and the European Society for Pediatric Gastroenterology, Hepatology, and Nutrition (ESPGHAN). *Journal of Pediatric Gastroenterology and Nutrition, 49,* 4, 498–547.

Yacob, D., & DiLorenzo, C. (2009). Functional abdominal pain: All roads lead to Rome (criteria). *Pediatric Annals, 38,* 5, 253–258.

8

Infectious Diseases

Jody K. Roblyer

Select one best answer to the following questions.

1. Sam's mother has telephoned the clinic because chicken pox has been "going around" at Sam's school and she has just noticed a few red spots along the hairline on his face. She asks if there is anything that can be given to shorten the duration or severity of the illness. Which of the following is most accurate?

   a. Diphenhydramine elixir has been shown to shorten the duration and severity of the rash.
   b. Acyclovir has been shown to shorten the duration and severity of the illness.
   c. Aspirin taken 4 times a day has been shown to shorten the duration and severity of the illness.
   d. There is no medication known to alter the course of the illness.

2. A 14-year-old adolescent has been diagnosed with mononucleosis. The PNP should teach the adolescent and the parents that which of the following should be avoided?

   a. Strenuous exercise if the spleen is palpable
   b. Weight-bearing activities until laboratory tests show resolution of the disease
   c. Unnecessary activity until lymph nodes return to normal size
   d. Stretching and reaching activities during the acute stage of illness

3. A well-nourished 10-year-old girl presents to the clinic with low-grade fever, sore throat, fatigue and malaise, and left upper abdominal pain. Based on clinical presentation and laboratory results, a diagnosis of infectious mononucleosis is made. Which of the presenting signs and symptoms requires further investigation immediately?

   a. Low-grade fever
   b. Sore throat with lymphadenopathy
   c. Fatigue and malaise
   d. Left upper abdominal pain

4. Initial treatment for a child with uncomplicated infectious mononucleosis should include:

   a. Home care with bed rest progressing to activity as tolerated
   b. Home care with complete bed rest until afebrile
   c. Hospitalization with complete bed rest until laboratory values return to normal
   d. Hospitalization with daily, planned physical therapy

5. You are performing a physical examination on a 12-year-old boy who is planning to go to summer camp in a primitive wooded area. What teaching is appropriate for the prevention of Rocky Mountain spotted fever?

   a. Inspect the body several times a day and remove ticks immediately.
   b. Inspect the skin while taking a shower and apply soap to ticks before removing.
   c. Ticks should be removed only after they have been killed with alcohol.
   d. Tick removal should be performed by a healthcare professional.

Questions 6, 7, and 8 refer to the following scenario.

The mother of 8-year-old John telephones to tell you that John developed chicken pox 3 days ago. She wants to know if there is anything she can do to make him more comfortable.

6. You should tell John's mother to:

   a. Apply topical calamine lotion
   b. Apply a topical antibiotic to the new vesicles
   c. Give aspirin for fever and discomfort
   d. Keep John out of bright light

7. You should also tell John's mother to:

   a. Avoid getting the lesions wet
   b. Encourage John to take a bath every day
   c. Have John take a bath only if he develops fever and sweats
   d. Encourage John to take only sponge baths until all lesions are healed

8. John's mother calls you again 10 days after onset of the initial rash to report that John has had a severe headache since yesterday and that he is very irritable. Which of the following would be advised?

   a. Ask the mother if John has had a bowel movement since he has been ill.
   b. Tell John's mother that these symptoms are common when chicken pox is resolving.
   c. Ask the mother if there is a family history of severe headaches.
   d. Ask John's mother to bring him to the office today for evaluation.

9. A 16-year-old boy has been diagnosed with measles (rubeola). He is also complaining of ear pain. His tympanic membranes are red and bulging. Appropriate management of the ear problem is to treat the ears with:

   a. Pain medication until the virus has run its course
   b. The same medication used to treat any case of otitis media
   c. Liquid topical antibiotics and topical steroids
   d. Acyclovir given by mouth

10. The mother of 7-year-old Bob has brought him to the clinic because he has a rash. Physical examination reveals vesicles on the hands, feet, and in the mouth. Hand, foot, and mouth disease is diagnosed. Treatment is based on:

    a. Alleviating symptoms
    b. Eradication of causative bacteria
    c. Prevention of febrile convulsions
    d. Prevention of secondary infections

11. The mother of 6-year-old Cali brings her to the clinic because the family is planning a trip to a tropical area, and

she wants to know how to avoid illness. Knowing that cases of malaria have been reported in the area, you should teach:

a. Avoidance of contact with infected people
b. Hand washing after touching contaminated fomites
c. Avoidance of mosquito bites
d. Cooking of all vegetables

12. Steven, at 6 years of age, has been diagnosed with erythema infectiosum (fifth disease). His mother asks you how to prevent the spread of the disease to her other children. Your answer should be:

a. The disease is not thought to be contagious.
b. Stephen should eat and drink from disposable containers.
c. Other children should not be allowed to touch the erythematous areas.
d. The patient is no longer contagious by the time the rash appears.

13. Considering the pathophysiology associated with erythema infectiosum (fifth disease), a child with history of which of the following diseases must be monitored closely?

a. Frequent respiratory infections
b. Multiple skin allergies
c. Malabsorption syndrome
d. Hemolytic anemia

14. The mother of 4-day-old Susan has brought her to the clinic because she has not seemed interested in her bottle since yesterday. Physical examination reveals a lethargic infant with an axillary temperature of 96°F and a pulse rate of 100. Extremities are slightly cool. Appropriate management includes:

a. Reassuring the mother that infants tend to regulate their own feeding habits
b. Instructing the mother on proper nipple placement and feeding techniques

c. Changing the infant to a soy-based formula and reevaluating her in 24 hours
d. Considering the possibility of sepsis with appropriate referral

15. The mother of a toddler with a typical roseola-type rash and a history of high fever asks if there is any treatment available for the condition. The PNP tells the mother that:

a. Topical corticosteroids are helpful to relieve itching
b. Oral diphenhydramine is helpful to decrease desquamation
c. Aspirin should be used to treat the typical high fever
d. There is no medical treatment for roseola

16. Mrs. Chancellor contracted rubella while pregnant with 1-month-old Andrew. Andrew should be considered contagious for what time period?

a. Between 5 and 7 days
b. Until he is afebrile
c. At least the first year of life
d. He is not contagious

17. James, at 4 years old, has been diagnosed with cat scratch disease. His mother asks what should be done about the cat. What should your response be?

a. The cat should be isolated until it can be treated with antibiotics.
b. The cat should be isolated until it can be treated with anthelmintics.
c. The cat should be evaluated by a medical laboratory and destroyed.
d. There are no recommendations for treating or destroying the cat.

18. Which of the following vaccines is contraindicated for routine use in a 3-year-old child who is receiving vincristine for maintenance treatment of acute lymphocytic leukemia?

a. DPT
b. Injectable influenza
c. MMR
d. Hepatitis B

19. Stephanie, at 1 year old, is infected with HIV, but is asymptomatic at this time. When should her MMR immunization be given?

    a. According to the usual schedule
    b. After she has been asymptomatic for 1 year
    c. Only if she attends day care
    d. MMR should not be given to Stephanie

20. Premature infants should receive routine immunizations based on:

    a. Chronologic age
    b. Gestational age
    c. Birth weight
    d. Current weight

21. Which of the following is recommended as the standard immunizing agent for healthy preschool children?

    a. DTP
    b. DTaP
    c. DT
    d. Td

◻ ANSWERS AND RATIONALE

1. **(b)** Acyclovir has been shown to slightly shorten the duration of fever and new lesion formation. Aspirin is not given to children with chicken pox because of its association with Reye's syndrome.

2. **(a)** To avoid splenic rupture, strenuous exercise and contact sports should be avoided as long as the spleen is palpable.

3. **(d)** Left upper abdominal pain should alert the practitioner to the possibility of splenic rupture. Sore throat should be cultured for strep if this has not been done (strep is a differential diagnosis for this presentation and strep often coexists with mono) but the need for the culture is not urgent.

4. **(a)** Bed rest and activity as tolerated are recommended in the initial treatment of uncomplicated infectious mononucleosis.

5. **(a)** Ticks must be attached for 4 to 6 hours or more before they can transmit Rocky Mountain spotted fever; frequent removal of ticks is valuable. Ticks do not need to be treated with soap or alcohol before removal, and do not need to be removed by a healthcare provider.

6. **(a)** Itching causes discomfort in children with chicken pox. Calamine lotion may be applied liberally for relief of itching caused by vesicular lesions. Neosporin does not decrease itching. Steroids may weaken the immune system and should not be used on the child with a herpes virus. Photophobia frequently occurs in rubeola (measles) but not chicken pox.

7. **(b)** There are no restrictions on bathing. Children with chicken pox should be encouraged to take daily baths to help prevent secondary bacterial infection, which is the most common complication of chicken pox.

8. **(d)** Cerebellar complications or cerebral infections may occur as a complication associated with chicken pox. These complications may occur 4 days preceding the rash until 3 weeks after the appearance of the rash. John's headache and irritability are signs that there may be an encephalopathy. John should be evaluated in the office to rule out this possibility.

9. **(b)** Otitis media is common with measles. It is treated as any acute otitis media.

10. **(a)** The course of hand, foot, and mouth disease (thought to be caused by a coxsackievirus) is usually benign and treatment is symptomatic. Fever is usually low grade and the throat is sore.

11. **(c)** The malaria parasite is spread by the mosquito bite.

12. **(d)** Erythema infectiosum is only contagious before the rash appears. The mode of transmission is thought to be respiratory secretions and blood.

13. **(d)** The profound reticulocytopenia associated with erythema infectiosum may result in a dangerous decrease of hemoglobin concentration in the child with hemolytic anemias such as sickle cell or thalassemia, pyruvate kinase deficiency, or acquired hemolytic anemia.

14. **(d)** The neonate with sepsis often presents with hypothermia, lethargy, poor feeding, and bradycardia. The nurse practitioner should refer for sepsis evaluation.

15. **(d)** There is no medical treatment for roseola. Febrile seizure is the most common complication of roseola, but the appearance of the diagnostic rash usually coincides with the abrupt termination of fever. Itching and desquamation are not associated with roseola.

16. **(c)** Infants with congenital rubella may excrete the virus from the nasopharynx and in the urine for a year.

17. **(d)** The capacity for disease transmission by cats appears to be transient. There are no recommendations for treating or destroying the cat. The cat may be declawed but the disease can also be induced by cat bites.

18. **(c)** MMR contains live virus vaccine and should not be given to a child (without consultation by a specialist) who is on immunosuppressive therapy, including chemotherapeutic agents such as vincristine.

19. **(b)** Pertussis immunization is not given routinely to children older than 7 years of age because severe pertussis is a disease of young children, and reaction to immunization appears to increase with age.

20. **(a)** Premature infants may be at greater risk for vaccine-preventable disease and should be immunized according to their chronologic age.

21. **(b)** DTaP is the standard immunizing agent for children younger than 7 years of age. DTP is an older formulation, and DT and Td both lack the important pertussis component but are used for adults and for children when pertussis is contraindicated.

◘ REFERENCES

American Academy of Pediatrics. (2006). *Red book: 2006 report of the committee on infectious diseases* (28th ed.). Elk Grove Village, IL: American Academy of Pediatrics.

Baraff, L. J. (2008). Management of infants and young children with fever without source. *Pediatric Annals, 37*, 10, 673–679.

Boynton, R. W., Dunn, E., & Stephens, G. R. (2009). *Manual of ambulatory pediatrics* (6th ed.). Baltimore, MD: Lippincott Williams & Wilkins.

Hay, W. W., Levin, M. J., Sondheimer, J. M., & Detarding, R. P. (2009). *Current diagnosis & treatment in pediatrics.* (19th ed.). New York, NY: McGraw-Hill.

Kane, K. S., Ryder, J. B., Johnson, R. A., Baden, H. P., & Stratigos, A. (2002). *Color atlas & synopsis of pediatric dermatology.* New York, NY: McGraw-Hill.

Shah, S. (2009). *Pediatric practice infectious diseases.* New York, NY: McGraw-Hill Companies.

Zitelli, B. J., & Davis, H. W. (2007). *Atlas of pediatric physical diagnosis.* Philadelphia, PA: Mosby.

9

Musculoskeletal Disorders

Rachel Lyons

Select one best answer for each of the following questions.

1. An injury at which of the following sites will most likely result in a bone length discrepancy?

   a. Diaphysis
   b. Epiphysis
   c. Medullary cavity
   d. Metaphysis

2. Growth in muscle length is related to growth in length of:

   a. Underlying bone
   b. Underlying ligament
   c. Underlying tendon
   d. Opposing muscle group

3. Varus between the tibia and femur of up to 15° followed by a progression to a neutral angle, which then progresses to valgus between 7° and 9°, is associated with which of the following?

   a. Blount disease
   b. Internal tibial torsion
   c. Normal developmental growth pattern
   d. Abnormal tibiofemoral growth pattern

4. Tracy, who is 9 years old, complains that she does not like to wear shorts because her knees look funny. Upon examination you note a genu valgum angle of greater than 15°. You should:

   a. Reevaluate in one year if still present
   b. Consult with an orthopedic specialist
   c. Instruct her to avoid the "W" sitting position
   d. Encourage exercise to strengthen quadriceps

5. What is the appropriate treatment for genu varum in a 15-month-old child?

   a. Passive exercise with each diaper change
   b. Denis Browne splint at night
   c. Blount brace at night
   d. No treatment is warranted

6. During examination of 2-week-old J. P., you note irritability when lifted, asymmetrical Moro reflex, and spasm along the right sternocleidomastoid. What does this suggest?

   a. Torticollis
   b. Sprengel deformity
   c. Fractured clavicle
   d. Klippel-Feil syndrome

7. A child with growing pains is most likely to experience:

   a. A mild limp
   b. Bilateral lower extremity pain
   c. Lower extremity pain primarily during the day
   d. Lower extremity pain associated with decreased range of motion

8. C. W., a 20-month-old, presents in the emergency room with a greenstick fracture of his left femur. Physical examination also reveals an enlarged anterior fontanel and enlarged costochondral junction. What do these clinical findings suggest?

   a. Child abuse
   b. Osteogenesis imperfecta
   c. Osteoporosis
   d. Rickets

9. Which of the following represents appropriate anticipatory guidance for a child diagnosed with slipped capital femoral epiphysis?

   a. Avoid contact sports until pain has resolved
   b. Crutches to facilitate mobility during acute phase
   c. Apply ice to affected area
   d. Range-of-motion and strengthening exercises

10. Which of the following factors most affects outcomes in patients with LCPD?

    a. Age
    b. Severity of pain and antalgic gait
    c. Family history of LCPD
    d. Bilateral involvement

11. During 2.5-year-old Jason's physical examination you note large, muscular-looking calves and observe his difficulty rising from a sitting position. The Denver screening examination reveals delays in the gross motor area. Which of the following laboratory tests would be most beneficial?

    a. Serum calcium
    b. Serum magnesium
    c. Serum phosphorus
    d. Serum creatine kinase

12. The appropriate management of Osgood-Schlatter's disease includes:

    a. Local injection of soluble corticosteroid
    b. Decreasing activity, applying ice, and taking NSAIDs
    c. Program of strengthening and stretching for quadriceps
    d. Casting in adduction for 6 weeks

13. You have been treating 14-month-old J. V. for torticollis since birth. The condition has not resolved. The appropriate management plan would be to:

    a. Refer for surgical consultation
    b. Continue with passive range of motion
    c. Provide environmental stimulation opposite the contracture
    d. Apply cervical collar at night

14. While completing the hip examination on a newborn infant you are able to dislocate the infant's right hip. The appropriate management plan would be to:

    a. Triple diaper and reevaluate in two weeks
    b. Recommend positioning prone while awake
    c. Refer to orthopedic specialist
    d. Order tight swaddling of the infant

15. Which of the following would not be an appropriate indicator for developmental dysplasia of the hip in a 6-month-old child?

    a. Allis sign
    b. Skinfold symmetry
    c. Galeazzi sign
    d. Ortolani maneuver

16. T. C., who is 3 years of age, presents with a history of fever for the past several days, pain in his left leg, and refusal to bear weight on the left leg. Ten days ago, he fell from a slide and bruised his leg. His WBC count is slightly elevated. You suspect

either toxic synovitis or osteomyelitis. Which finding supports a diagnosis of osteomyelitis more so than toxic synovitis?

a. Recent injury
b. Leg pain
c. Nonweight bearing
d. Elevated WBC

17. Which of the following suggests internal tibial torsion rather than internal femoral torsion in a 2-year-old child presenting with an in-toeing gait?

a. Sitting in "W" position
b. Knees face forward when walking
c. Generalized ligament laxity
d. Limited external rotation of hip

18. You examine C. J. in the newborn nursery and note a deformity in her left foot consisting of a convex lateral border and a forefoot, which can be abducted past an imaginary line extending from the middle of the heel through the second toe. Which of the following management strategies is most appropriate?

a. Reverse last shoes
b. Out flare shoes
c. Stretching exercises
d. Orthopedic referral

19. A macular, salmon to red colored rash with irregular borders and central clearing is typical of which of the following?

a. Systemic juvenile arthritis
b. Lyme disease
c. Systemic lupus erythematosus
d. Rheumatic fever

20. Coach Jones asks for advice on how to prevent Little League elbow in his 8- and 9-year-old players. Which of the following would be an incorrect advice?

a. Have each child pitch only three innings
b. Limit or eliminate curve balls
c. Use ice massage before and after pitching
d. Conduct slow warm-ups

◘ ANSWERS AND RATIONALE

1. **(b)** Bone length occurs at the epiphyseal plates, which is also where the blood supply enters. If the blood supply is compromised growth may be jeopardized.

2. **(a)** Growth in muscles is due to the range of motion the muscle is asked to perform as the underlying bone lengthens.

3. **(c)** The normal growth pattern is one of slight varus (bowleg), which progresses to a neutral angle and then slight valgus (knock-knee). Persistence of any phase beyond what is expected warrants further investigation.

4. **(a)** Valgus up to 15° is common up through the age of 8 or 9 years but persistence beyond that may lead to problems and degenerative changes, and warrants referral.

5. **(d)** Genu varum, or bowed leg, is normal until approximately 18 months.

6. **(c)** A fractured clavicle is not an uncommon finding following birth, especially in large babies. The spasm of the sternocleidomastoid and asymmetrical Moro reflex are classic signs of this problem.

7. **(b)** Growing pains tend to occur during rapid growth, increasing in prevalence after 5 years of age. The pain is a muscular pain located bilaterally in the legs and thighs.

8. **(d)** Rickets develops after several months of vitamin D deficiency and is characterized by craniotabes and enlarged anterior fontanel with delayed closing. The enlarged costochondral junction, or rachitic rosary, is a classic sign.

9. **(b)** Treatment of slipped capital femoral epiphysis is aimed at preventing further slippage. Since the goal is no weight bearing and avoiding flexion of the hip, no sports

are recommended. Ice would not change the problem in the femoral head, and ROM and exercise are contraindicated.

10. **(a)** Age, because younger children have more time to remodel compared with older children. Severity of pain, antalgic gait, family history, or bilateral involvement all have less impact on outcome than does age.

11. **(d)** Creatinine is formed in healthy muscle tissue from creatine at a steady rate. When muscle wasting occurs, as in muscular dystrophy, creatine excretion is dramatically increased. Deficiencies in serum calcium, phosphorus, and magnesium may result in muscle cramping and spasms but do not represent the clinical picture described.

12. **(b)** Osgood-Schlatter's disease is a benign condition resulting from overuse and is best treated with rest and supportive therapy.

13. **(a)** Most torticollis resolves by 1 year of age. When there is no response to more conservative treatment interventions such as passive stretching and environmental stimulation, surgery is the recommended course of action.

14. **(c)** Although still recommended in some sources, triple diapering is not thought to be effective because the musculoskeletal forces are greater than those exerted by diapers. Swaddling and the prone position are contraindicated and may increase the risk of dislocation. The appropriate treatment would be an evaluation by an orthopedic specialist and most likely a Pavlik harness.

15. **(d)** After the age of 6 months, the Ortolani maneuver is less reliable due to diminished laxity in the hip. After 2 months of age, soft tissue contractures may develop, making this test unreliable.

16. **(a)** Osteomyelitis is frequently associated with local trauma, whereas toxic synovitis is more commonly associated with a recent upper respiratory illness.

17. **(b)** Observing the patella can be very helpful in differentiating internal tibial torsion from internal femoral torsion. The patella will rotate inward if the problem is above the knee. There is also general ligamentous laxity in other areas (fingers, elbows) associated with internal tibial torsion.

18. **(c)** Metatarsus adductus is a flexural deformity of the foot related most commonly to intrauterine positioning. Flexible deformities, that is, movement past the midline, can be managed with stretching exercises.

19. **(a)** This is the characteristic rash associated with systemic juvenile arthritis that occurs in 25 to 50% of children.

20. **(c)** Little League elbow or epicondylitis is a result of repetitive forearm supination and pronation. Therefore, the goal is to prevent the injury by reducing the repetitive motion. Ice falsely reassures parent or coach that the injury can be prevented by applying before and after pitching.

◘ REFERENCES

Behrman, R. E., & Kliegman, R. M. (Eds.). (2002). *Nelson essentials of pediatrics* (4th ed.). Philadelphia, PA: W. B. Saunders.

Burns, B. E., Brady, M., Dunn, A. M., & Starr, N. (Eds.). (2000). *Pediatric primary care: A handbook for nurse practitioners.* Philadelphia, PA: W. B. Saunders.

Fox, J. A. (Ed.). (2000). *Primary health care of children* (2nd ed.). St. Louis, MO: Mosby.

Hay, W. W., Hayward, A. R., Levin, M. J., & Sondheimer, J. M. (Eds.). (2003). *Current pediatric diagnosis and treatment* (16th ed.). New York, NY: Lange Medical Books/McGraw-Hill.

10

Neurologic Disorders

Maureen Maguire

Select one best answer to the following questions.

1. A 5-month-old boy, a former 28-week-premature infant, is being evaluated in your practice because of a concern about delayed motor development. In formulating the differential diagnosis, you keep in mind that spastic cerebral palsy is characterized by:

   a. Increased deep tendon reflexes and sustained clonus
   b. Dystonic posturing
   c. Abnormal involuntary movements
   d. Nystagmus

2. A 4-year-old child with a history of myelomeningocele and a ventriculoperitoneal shunt presents to the clinic with a headache, nausea, vomiting, and lethargy. The most probable diagnosis is:

   a. Viral gastroenteritis
   b. Shunt malfunction
   c. Meningitis
   d. Shunt infection

3. An apparently healthy child, who is enrolled in Head Start, is suspected of having developmental delays based on Denver II results at two separate clinic visits. The most appropriate next step would be to:

   a. Request developmental evaluation from the Head Start program
   b. Repeat the Denver II in 6 months
   c. Refer the child for a more definitive evaluation
   d. Discuss ways in which parents can foster the child's development

4. Amanda is a 6-month-old infant recovering from a viral illness. At the peak of her illness (2 days ago), she spiked a temperature of 104°F and experienced a febrile seizure. Amanda's mother is young and inexperienced, but is very open to teaching. She wants to know if the seizure will "do anything" to Amanda. While teaching this new mother about simple febrile seizures, it would be accurate to say that Amanda:

   a. Is at increased risk for epilepsy as an adult
   b. Would benefit from phenytoin prophylaxis
   c. May experience repeated seizures
   d. Would benefit from phenobarbital prophylaxis

5. Which of the following signs is not characteristic of generalized seizures?

   a. Unilateral motor manifestations
   b. Disturbance of consciousness
   c. Tonic stiffening of the trunk
   d. Simultaneous and symmetric cerebral hemisphere discharge

6. Which of the following is the primary diagnostic tool used in the evaluation of seizure disorder?

   a. EEG
   b. Cerebral blood flow studies
   c. CT scan
   d. MRI

7. Upon physical examination of a 4-year-old boy, you note seven café au lait spots greater than 5 mm in diameter. This finding may be indicative of:

   a. Tuberous sclerosis
   b. Sturge-Weber disease
   c. Duchenne's dystrophy
   d. Neurofibromatosis

8. Michael is a 15-year-old high school student who presents for a school sports physical. He appears to be in good health, but is concerned about a bad headache he had a few weeks ago. He is concerned because his mother's friend died of a brain tumor. You tell Michael that the most common type of headache with onset in adolescence is:

   a. Sinus headache
   b. Vascular headache
   c. Tension headache
   d. Migraine headache

9. An 18-year-old college freshman is seen in the student clinic with a complaint of migraine headaches. In collecting the history, you would expect him to say he experiences pain:

   a. Throughout his head without any localization
   b. Restricted to one side of his head during an episode
   c. Mostly in the occipital area
   d. Across his head from one temporal side to another

10. Which of the following historic points would not alert the practitioner to the possibility of a brain tumor?

    a. Headache in the morning associated with vomiting
    b. Failure to thrive and developmental delay in young children
    c. School failure and personality changes in older children
    d. Sleep apnea

11. Which of the following signs is not scored in the Glasgow Coma Scale?

    a. Eye opening
    b. Verbal response
    c. Upper limb response
    d. Fine motor response

12. Mr. Harris calls the pediatric clinic to say that Josh, his 2-year-old son, has tripped on the sidewalk and hit his head on concrete. Which of the following symptoms reported by Mr. Harris would require that Josh be seen in the emergency room?

    a. Uncontrollable crying
    b. Loss of consciousness
    c. Scalp laceration
    d. History of febrile seizures

13. A 2-year-old child is evaluated in the emergency department for a closed head injury following a 10-foot fall from an open window. When interpreting diagnostic imaging results, you are aware that the most common and generally the least serious type of skull fracture is:

    a. Basilar fracture
    b. Compound fracture
    c. Depressed fracture
    d. Linear fracture

14. A 12-month-old child, whose parents have a history of noncompliance for routine care, presents to the clinic with fever, irritability, and nuchal rigidity. The most critical diagnostic step in the child with suspected meningitis is:

    a. The history
    b. The physical examination
    c. Evaluation of the CSF
    d. Blood culture

15. In a child with suspected meningitis, the lumbar puncture should be delayed and a CT scan obtained first in which of the following circumstances?

    a. There are signs of increased intracranial pressure.
    b. The child has tachycardia.
    c. The child has a negative Brudzinski sign.
    d. The WBC count is greater than $10,000/mm^3$.

16. Primary immunization is of paramount importance for preventing meningitis especially in young children that is caused by:

    a. *Haemophilus influenzae* type b
    b. *Neisseria meningitidis*
    c. *Escherichia coli*
    d. *Klebsiella pneumonia*

17. The most common type of brain tumor in children is:

    a. Ependymoma
    b. Brain stem tumor
    c. Craniopharyngioma
    d. Medulloblastoma

18. In most states, a learning disability is defined based on:

    a. The child's IQ as determined by a psychological evaluation
    b. A discrepancy between the child's actual and expected achievement
    c. A diagnosis of attention deficits
    d. Achievement test scores

19. Which of the following is a measure of childhood intelligence?

    a. Wechsler scales
    b. Denver II
    c. Bayley scales
    d. Vineland scales

20. In working with a child with Tourette syndrome and his family, the nurse practitioner should be aware that:

    a. Symptoms become more unpredictable during adolescence.
    b. Boys are more likely than girls to exhibit behavioral problems such as obsessive–compulsive disorder.
    c. Sleep disturbance from tics increases with age.
    d. There are several medications now available to control the tics without interfering with daily functioning.

21. There are several skin features seen with tuberous sclerosis. Which of the following is most characteristic?

    a. Café au lait spots
    b. Blue or purple striae
    c. Papules in a "Christmas tree" pattern
    d. Hypopigmented macules in an "ash leaf" shape

ANSWERS AND RATIONALE

1. **(a)** In spastic CP, a lowered reflex threshold results in increased DTRs and sustained clonus. The other signs are characteristic of dyskinetic and ataxic CP.

2. **(b)** Headache, nausea, vomiting, and lethargy are frequently associated with malfunctioning shunt systems.

3. **(c)** If a developmental lag is suspected based on repeated performances on the Denver II (which is a screening tool), a more definitive assessment should be obtained.

4. **(c)** Children with a diagnosis of simple febrile seizures may experience repeated febrile seizures, particularly if the first seizure occurred before 1 year of age. They are not at increased risk for epilepsy as adults, phenytoin is not efficacious as a prophylactic drug, and phenobarbital is not routinely recommended.

5. **(a)** In generalized seizures, motor manifestations, if any, are bilateral.

6. **(a)** In the study of seizure disorders, the EEG has the greatest clinical applicability. The other imaging techniques are considered supplemental.

7. **(d)** More than six café au lait spots (greater than 5 mm in diameter) in prepubertal children is an essential part of the diagnosis of neurofibromatosis.

8. **(c)** The most common headache in adolescents is the tension, or psychogenic, headache.

9. **(b)** After puberty, migraine headache pain is restricted to one side of the head but may switch sides from one headache episode to another.

10. **(d)** Brain tumors can be associated with morning headaches, vomiting, and behavioral changes. Sleep apnea is associated with airway obstruction or other neuromuscular disorders.

11. **(d)** The Glasgow Coma Scale is based on eye opening, verbal response, and best upper limb response.

12. **(b)** Emergency care should be sought following head trauma if the child is unresponsive.

13. **(d)** The linear fracture is the most common and has little serious clinical implication, unless it overlies a vascular channel or penetrates an air sinus.

14. **(c)** Collection of the CSF is the most critical diagnostic step in the child with suspected meningitis, based on the history and physical examination.

15. **(a)** If elevated intracranial pressure is suspected, a CT scan should be obtained first to avoid the complication of cerebellar or uncal herniation.

16. **(a)** Recommended primary immunization schedules include vaccines licensed for use against *H. influenzae* type b.

17. **(d)** Medulloblastomas are the most common brain tumors of childhood.

18. **(b)** In most states, a learning disability means a discrepancy between the child's actual and expected achievement.

19. **(a)** The Wechsler scales measure intelligence, the Denver and Bayley measure development, and the Vineland measures adaptive behavior.

20. **(a)** Changing hormones make the symptoms more unpredictable.

21. **(d)** Hypopigmented macules in an elliptical shape are characteristic and are often described as "ash leaf" spot.

◻ REFERENCES

American Psychiatric Association. (2000). *Diagnostic and statistical manual of mental disorders* (4th ed.). Washington, DC: Author.

Berman, S. (2006). *Pediatric decision-making* (4th ed.). St. Louis, MO: Mosby.

Custer, J. W., Rau, R. E., & Lee, C. K. (Eds.). (2008). *The Harriet Lane handbook* (18th ed.). St. Louis, MO: Elsevier Health Services.

Engel, J. (2006). Report of the ILAE classification core group. *Epilepsia, 47*, 1558–1568.

Farley, J. A. (2004). Epilepsy. In J. Allen, & J. A. Vessey (Eds.). *Primary care of a child with a chronic condition* (5th ed.). St. Louis: Mosby.

Hockenberry, M. J. (2003). *Wong's nursing care of infants and children.* (8th ed.). St. Louis, MO: Mosby.

Hoekelman, R. A., Adam, H. M., Nelson, N. M., Weitzman, M. L., & Wilson, M. H. (Eds.). (2001). *Primary pediatric care* (4th ed.). St. Louis, MO: Mosby.

Kliegman, R., Behman, R., Jenson, H. B., & Stanton, B. (Eds.). (2007). *Nelson textbook of pediatrics* (18th ed.). Philadelphia, PA: W. B. Saunders.

Levine, M. D., Carey, W. B., & Croder, A. C. (Eds.). (1999). *Developmental-behavioral pediatrics* (3rd ed.). Philadelphia, PA: W. B. Saunders.

Marx, J. A. (Ed.). (2006). *Rosen's emergency medicine: Current concepts and clinical practice* (6th ed.). St. Louis, MO: Mosby.

Mason, J. R. (2008). Brain tumor—children. In *A.D.A.M. Medical Encyclopedia*. Available at: http://www.nlm.nih.gov/medlineplus/print/ency/article/000768.htm. Accessed May 22, 2009.

Mayo Clinic Staff. (2008). *Headaches in children*. Available at: http://www.mayoclinic.com/health/headaches-in-children/DS01132/METHOD=print&DS. Accessed May 2, 2009.

National Institute of Neurological Disorders and Stroke. (2009). *Neurofibromatosis fact sheet*. Available at: http://www.ninds.nih.gov/disorders/neurofibromatosis/detail_neurofibromatosis.htm?css=. Accessed May 19, 2009.

Pellock, J. M., Dodson, W. E., & Bourgeois, B. F. D. (Eds.). (2001). *Pediatric epilepsy diagnosis and therapy* (2nd ed.). New York, NY: DEMOS.

Roach, E. S., & Delgado, M. P. (1995). Tuberous Sclerosis. *Dermatologic Clinics, 13*, 151–161.

Schutzman, S. A. (2005). Injuries—head. In G. R. Fleisher, S. Ludwig, & F. M. Henretig (Eds.) *Textbook of pediatric emergency medicine* (5th ed.). Philadelphia, PA: Lippincott Williams & Wilkins

11

Genitourinary and Gynecologic Conditions

MaryLou C. Rosenblatt and Marlo Eldridge

Select one best answer to the following questions.

Questions 1 and 2 refer to the following scenario.

A 10-year-old boy comes to your clinic for evaluation of a suspected urinary tract infection (UTI).

1. Which of the following signs would lead you to include diagnoses other than UTI in the differential?

    a. Increased frequency
    b. Penile discharge
    c. Costovertebral tenderness
    d. Dysuria

2. The culture indicates sensitivity to tri-methoprim/sulfamethoxazole. The boy is treated with this antibiotic for 10 days. The most appropriate follow-up in this case would include:

    a. Obtaining a urinalysis in 2 weeks
    b. Instructing the parents that the child should return to the clinic if symptoms persist
    c. Teaching parents home monitoring with nitrite sticks
    d. Referring the child for a renal ultrasound

3. The most important laboratory test to be performed when a UTI is suspected in a school-age child is a:

    a. CBC with differential
    b. Urine dipstick
    c. Clean catch urine for U/A and C/S
    d. Voiding cystourethrogram (VCUG)

4. Jay is a 9-year-old boy who has had no significant health problems by history, but his mother is very concerned because he is "wetting himself." As you begin your history and physical examination, you keep in mind that the most common type of enuresis in school-age children is:

    a. Primary nocturnal enuresis
    b. Occasional daytime enuresis
    c. Secondary nocturnal enuresis
    d. Primary diurnal enuresis

5. Which of the following statements is not true with regard to primary nocturnal enuresis?

    a. There is often a positive family history of enuresis.
    b. It appears to be related to maturational delay.
    c. Some nighttime wetters stop wetting without any form of treatment.
    d. The incidence is higher in girls than in boys.

6. Which of the following is not true about the use of imipramine for the treatment of enuresis?

    a. It is not generally recommended for this nonfatal disorder due to the potentially lethal side effects.
    b. The lasting cure rate is approximately 17%.
    c. Imipramine should only be given to children who have had a baseline EEG.
    d. The most appropriate imipramine treatment group is adolescent boys with both ADHD and persistent nocturnal enuresis.

7. While examining a 4-month-old boy, you are unable to palpate one of the testes. The next most appropriate step is to:

    a. Reassure the parents that this is a normal finding
    b. Refer the child to an endocrinologist
    c. Reexamine the baby in 2 months
    d. Refer the child to a urologist

8. Which of the following is not true with regard to hypospadias?

    a. The meatus is formed along the dorsum of the penis.
    b. It is one of the most common penile abnormalities.
    c. Circumcision should be deferred.
    d. A referral for an endocrine evaluation may be indicated.

9. Upon examination of a 2-month-old boy, you notice a swelling in the right inguinal canal. Your differential diagnosis would not include:

    a. Diastasis recti
    b. Hydrocele of the spermatic cord
    c. Inguinal hernia
    d. Lymphadenopathy

Questions 10 and 11 refer to the following scenario.

A 12-year-old girl presents to your clinic with symptoms of vaginitis, including odor, dysuria, frequency, and discomfort.

10. Which of the following causes of vaginitis is most likely due to sexual transmission?

    a. Candida
    b. Chlamydia
    c. Pinworms
    d. Gardnerella

11. Upon further history, physical examination, and laboratory screening, the girl is diagnosed with *Candida albicans* vaginitis. Appropriate treatment would include:

    a. Avoiding bubble baths
    b. Topical acyclovir
    c. Ceftriaxone
    d. Clotrimazole

12. A labial adhesion extending from the posterior fourchette to the clitoris is noted during the routine assessment of a 4-year-old girl. There is no history of difficulty voiding, dysuria, or discomfort. The most appropriate initial management is to:

    a. Recommend mechanical lysis using petrolatum ointment
    b. Prescribe a topical application of estrogen cream
    c. Refer to a GU specialist
    d. Reassure parents that no specific treatment is needed at this time

13. Patients with acute nephrotic syndrome may present with all but which of the following signs?

    a. Edema
    b. Hypertension
    c. Dark amber-colored urine
    d. History of weight loss

14. It is important to look for evidence of a preceding streptococcal infection when ruling out acute nephritis. This is best done by:

    a. Throat culture
    b. Skin examination
    c. ASO titer
    d. ESR

15. An adolescent boy presents to the clinic with a painless mass in the left side of his scrotum. The most likely diagnosis is:

    a. Epididymitis
    b. Testicular torsion
    c. Incarcerated hernia
    d. Hydrocele

16. A foul-smelling vaginal discharge that emits a fishy odor when combined with 10% potassium hydroxide is most likely due to:

    a. *Gardnerella vaginalis*
    b. *Candida albicans*
    c. *Chlamydia trachomatis*
    d. *N. gonorrhoeae*

17. A 17-year-old, sexually active girl with chancres in the genital area is noted to have a positive Venereal Disease Research Laboratories (VDRL) test. The next step should be to:

    a. Treat with ceftriaxone
    b. Perform a specific treponemal anti-body test
    c. Culture for *C. trachomatis*
    d. Discuss safer sex practices

18. The most common bacterial cause of a sexually transmitted infection (STI) is:

    a. *Neisseria gonorrhoeae*
    b. *Trichomonas vaginalis*
    c. *Chlamydia trachomatis*
    d. Herpes simplex

19. Which of the following is an absolute contraindication for use of combined hormonal contraceptives in adolescent women:

    a. History of thromboembolism
    b. Diabetes
    c. Smokes five cigarettes per day
    d. Sickle cell disease

20. A 15-year-old girl, who had menarche at 13 years of age, complains of monthly menstrual pain on the first day of her periods for 1 year. She has never been sexually active. Which of the following is not a characteristic of dysmenorrhea?

    a. Increased production of uterine prostaglandins
    b. Pain usually starts within hours of menstrual flow or may precede flow by up to 2 days
    c. Anovulatory cycles
    d. Crampy, spasmodic pain in the lower abdominal area, which might radiate to inner thighs

21. Which of the following is a risk factor for adolescent pregnancy?

    a. Good grades in school
    b. Asks for contraceptive at the school health clinic
    c. Plans to study nursing in college
    d. Unsure if monogamous partner uses condoms

22. Cara is a 16-year-old adolescent who has been sexually active with a male partner for 6 months. They have used condoms consistently. Cara is interested in a hormonal method as well. Your advice includes all of the following except:

    a. Combined oral contraceptives prevent ovulation.
    b. Transdermal contraceptive patches must be correctly applied and the site rotated.
    c. The vaginal contraceptive ring must be changed weekly.
    d. Long-acting progestins might cause weight gain.

23. Dan is a healthy 17-year-old student. He is thinking about having sex, but asks for more information about condoms. You give him all of the following advice except:

    a. Male condoms are the most effective barrier method.
    b. Latex condoms are the most recommended and are heat tolerant.
    c. Condoms have a theoretical failure rate of 3%.
    d. It is only safe to use water-based lubricant with latex condoms.

◻ ANSWERS AND RATIONALE

1. **(b)** Classic signs of a UTI include enuresis, frequency, dysuria, urgency, fever, and CVA tenderness. Discharge may indicate balanitis or a sexually transmitted disease.

2. **(d)** Older boys with a first infection should be examined for urinary tract abnormalities. The other laboratory tests do not assess for urinary tract anomalies.

3. **(c)** A clean catch midstream collection of urine is usually satisfactory to obtain a specimen for culture and sensitivity.

4. **(a)** Primary nocturnal enuresis occurs in 90% of enuretic children (e.g., they are wet only at night during sleep and have never had a sustained period of dryness).

5. **(d)** The incidence of primary nocturnal enuresis is three times higher in boys than in girls.

6. **(c)** Imipramine use is controversial due to dangerous side effects and its relative ineffectiveness. An EEG is not recommended prior to initiating treatment.

7. **(c)** If spontaneous descent of the testis does not occur by 12 months of age, surgical correction is indicated to reduce the risk of infertility.

8. **(a)** In hypospadias, the meatus opens on the ventral surface. In epispadias, which occurs less frequently, the opening is along the dorsal surface.

9. **(a)** Diastasis recti is a midline fascial attenuation extending from the umbilicus to the xiphoid process.

10. **(b)** Papillomas, trichomonas, herpes simplex, gonococcal, and chlamydial disease carry a high suspicion for sexual transmission. Candida typically occurs after a course of antibiotics, Gardnerella is indigenous vaginal flora, and pinworms is a parasitic disease.

11. **(d)** In *Candida albicans*, local application of clotrimazole, miconazole, and ticonazole appear to be equally effective.

12. **(d)** If there is no evidence of UTI, obstruction, or discomfort, and parents are not unusually concerned, then no treatment is necessary. Estrogen cream may be initiated if treatment is urgently desired by the parents in spite of counseling. Spontaneous resolution usually occurs in a manner of months and is more effective than surgical or mechanical lysis.

13. **(d)** Children with nephrotic syndrome typically present with edema and inappropriate weight gain.

14. **(c)** The antistreptolysin O (ASO) titer is elevated in 80% of patients with a preceding streptococcal infection.

15. **(d)** A hydrocele is not associated with pain, but the other suggested diagnoses are associated with pain.

16. **(a)** Bacterial vaginosis, often caused by an overgrowth of *Gardnerella vaginosis*, is suspected on the basis of a malodorous vaginal discharge and positive "whiff" test when mixing the discharge with potassium hydroxide.

17. **(b)** If the VDRL is positive, a specific treponemal test such as FTA-ABs should be done to confirm the diagnosis. Treatment is with benzathine penicillin G.

18. **(c)** Chlamydia is the most common bacterial cause of STD with over 4 million cases annually.

19. **(a)** Estrogen containing combined hormonal contraceptives increase hepatic production of extrinsic clotting factors and increase the relative risk for thromboembolic events in women with a h/o DVT/PE.

20. **(c)** Primary dysmenorrhea usually begins within 1 to 3 years of menarche and is associated with the establishment of ovulatory cycles.

21. **(d)** Poor communication with one's partner is a definite risk factor for adolescent pregnancy.

22. **(c)** The vaginal contraceptive ring is worn for 3 weeks, removed, and then a new ring is inserted 1 week later.

23. **(b)** Heat can cause latex condoms to break down.

◘ REFERENCES

American Academy of Pediatrics. (2009). *Red book: 2009 report of the committee on infectious diseases* (28th ed.). Elk Grove Village, IL: American Academy of Pediatrics.

Behrman, R. E., Kliegman, R. M., & Jenson, H. B. (Eds.). (2007). Nelson textbook of pediatrics (18th ed.). Philadelphia, PA: W. B. Saunders.

Berkowitz, C. D. (Ed.). (2008). Pediatrics: A primary care approach (3rd ed.). Philadelphia, PA: W. B. Saunders.

Burns, C. E., Dunn, A. M., Brady, M. A., Starr, N. B., & Blosser, C. (Eds.). (2008). *Pediatric primary care* (4th ed.). St. Louis, MO: Elsevier Saunders.

Emans, S. J., Laufer, M. R., & Goldstein, D. P. (Eds.). (2005). Pediatric and adolescent gynecology (5th ed.). Philadelphia, PA: Lippincott-Raven.

Guttmacher Institute (2006). Facts on American Teens' Sexual and Reproductive Health. Available at: http://www.guttmacher.org/pubs/fb_ATSRH.html. Accessed June 30, 2009.

Hatcher, R. A., Trussell, J., Stewart, F., Cates, W., Jr., Stewart, G. K., Guest, F., & Kowal, D. (2004). *Contraceptive technology* (18th ed.). New York, NY: Ardent Media.

Kim S., Lee J. W., Park J., Na, K. Y., Joo, K. W., Ahn, C., *et al.* (2004). The urine-blood PCO2 gradient as a diagnostic index of H (+) –ATPase defect distal renal tubular acidosis. *Kidney International, 66,* 761–767.

Kliegman, R. M., Behrman, R. E., Jenson, H. B., & Stanton, B. M. D. (Eds.). (2007). *Nelson textbook of pediatrics* (18th ed.). Philadelphia, PA: W. B. Saunders.

Koo, H. P. (2001). Is it really cryptorchism? *Contemporary Urology, 13,* 1, 12–18.

March of Dimes. (2009). *Teenage pregnancy* (Quick reference: Fact sheet) Available at: http://www.marchofdimes.com/professionals/14332_1159.asp. Accessed June 29, 2009.

Meade, C. S., & Ickovics, J. R. (2005). Systemic review of sexual risk among pregnant and mothering teens in the USA. *Social Science and Medicine, 60,* 4, 661–678.

Neinstein, L. S. (2008). Adolescent health care: A practical guide (5th ed.). Philadelphia, PA: Wolters Kluwer/Lippincott Williams & Wilkins.

Schwartz G. J., Al-Awati, Q. (2005). Role of hensin in mediating the adaptation of the cortical collecting duct to metabolic acidosis. *Current Opinion in Nephrology and Hypertension, 14,* 4, 383–388.

Yin Sinhoe, J. D., Wong, S., & Yeung, C. K. (2005). Voiding disorders. In D. F. Geary, & F. Schaefer (Eds.). *Comprehensive pediatric nephrology* (pp. 587–606). Philadelphia, PA: Mosby.

Hematologic Disorders

M. Elizabeth Younger

Select one best answer to the following questions.

1. A 3-year-old boy with known glucose-6-phosphate dehydrogenase (G6PD) deficiency has acute purulent otitis media. Which of the following drugs should not be used for his treatment?

   a. Amoxicillin
   b. Amoxicillin-clavulanate
   c. Erythromycin
   d. Trimethoprim/sulfamethoxazole

2. Mrs. C. has brought her 2-year-old daughter April to the clinic with complaints of anorexia and irritability for the past several weeks. You note that she is afebrile and appears pale. Based on the signs and symptoms, which initial action is appropriate?

   a. Ask Mrs. C. to describe April's diet, including the specific foods she is eating, prior to the onset of these symptoms.
   b. Prescribe supplemental iron therapy to be given three times a day.
   c. Order laboratory work to assess red blood cell count and indices.
   d. Refer April to a pediatrician for further evaluation.

3. Mrs. B. has brought 5-year-old Julio to the clinic. She reports that he has been lethargic and has been running a low-grade fever for about 2 weeks. Physical examination reveals no significant findings other than pallor and lymphadenopathy. A complete blood count reveals a decreased hematocrit, neutropenia, and thrombocytopenia. The practitioner's next action should be to:

   a. Prescribe a broad spectrum antibiotic and ferrous sulfate
   b. Instruct Mrs. B. on the appropriate use of acetaminophen to treat Julio's fever
   c. Reassure Mrs. B. that Julio's signs and symptoms are indicative of a viral infection
   d. Refer Julio to a pediatric hematologist/oncologist for further evaluation

4. Routine laboratory studies have revealed that a 2-year-old child has a decreased level of serum ferritin. Red cell count and indices are within normal limits for age. Based on this information, you may assume that the child:

   a. May have stage 1 iron deficiency anemia
   b. Likely has stage 2 iron deficiency anemia
   c. Likely has stage 3 iron deficiency anemia
   d. Does not have any stage of anemia

5. You have ordered red blood cell indices for a 10-year-old girl. Results reveal a decrease in both the mean corpuscular hemoglobin (MCH) and the mean corpuscular volume (MCV). Differential diagnosis should include:

   a. Sickle cell anemia
   b. Vitamin B_{12} deficiency anemia
   c. Pernicious anemia
   d. Iron deficiency anemia

6. When planning screening protocols, it is important for the practitioner to know that iron deficiency anemia is most common in which life period(s)?

   a. The first month of life
   b. The period when the child is most sedentary
   c. The preschool years
   d. Periods of rapid growth

7. The PNP is teaching high school students about prevention of iron deficiency anemia. To teach prevention of the most common cause of iron deficiency in this age group, it is important to emphasize:

   a. Avoidance of all aspirin containing products
   b. A diet high in iron-rich foods
   c. Avoidance of ingestion of carbonated beverages
   d. Avoidance of high-fiber foods

8. You have prescribed iron supplements for a 3-year-old child. When instructing the parents about how to give the iron preparation, it is important to tell them that iron:

   a. Is best absorbed on an empty stomach
   b. Is best absorbed when given with meals
   c. Is best absorbed when given with milk
   d. Should not be given near bedtime

9. One month after prescribing iron therapy to treat iron deficiency in a child who has no other known health problems, the PNP should:

   a. Teach the parent or guardian about iron-rich foods
   b. Check the child's stools for occult blood
   c. Order a hemoglobin measurement
   d. Order a complete blood count

10. After treating a 2-year-old for iron deficiency anemia, laboratory tests show that his hemoglobin level has returned to normal. Which of the following actions is appropriate?

    a. Discontinue iron therapy and recheck his hemoglobin level in 1 month.
    b. Discontinue iron therapy and tell the child's mother to reinitiate therapy if she notices any pallor.
    c. Continue iron therapy until all the medicine at home is gone.
    d. Continue iron therapy for 2 to 3 months.

11. Jackson was born at 34 weeks gestation. He is now 10 weeks old and his mother has brought him to your office for a routine examination. He appears alert and well developed. His mother tells you that he takes 2 to 4 oz. of formula every 2 to 4 hours around the clock. The plan for Jackson should include which of the following?

    a. Initiation of rice cereal at bedtime
    b. Addition of two bottles of water each day

c. Encouraging Jackson's mother to limit his feedings to every 4 to 6 hours

d. Prescribing ferrous sulfate to be administered three times a day

12. While evaluating the complete blood count (CBC) results of a 3-year-old child, the practitioner notes that in addition to hypochromia and micro-cytosis of the red cell, there are many poikilocytes and target cells. Based on this finding, differential diagnosis must include:

a. Thalassemia major
b. Iron deficiency anemia
c. Pernicious anemia
d. Vitamin B_{12} deficiency

13. When laboratory results reveal a hypochromic, microcytic anemia in a 2-year-old child, differential diagnosis must include:

a. Lead poisoning
b. Pernicious anemia
c. Hemophilia
d. Folic acid deficiency

14. The mother of a well-developed, full-term 3-week-old boy brings him to the clinic because he has been fussy and not eating well for the past week. A CBC reveals that he is anemic. When exploring the etiology of the anemia, it is important to know that which of the following is not a common cause of anemia in the newborn?

a. Dietary iron deficiency
b. Blood loss
c. Hemolysis
d. Decreased RBC production

15. To establish a diagnosis of sickle cell disease, which laboratory test is appropriate?

a. CBC with RBC indices
b. Sickle cell prep
c. Sickledex
d. Hemoglobin electrophoresis

Questions 16, 17, and 18 refer to the following scenario.

Tonya, at 5 years of age, has sickle cell disease.

16. To decrease the risk of vaso-occlusive crises, it is important to stress which of the following to Tonya and her parents?

a. The need for frequent hand washing
b. The need for a diet high in iron
c. Avoidance of the use of mothballs in the house
d. Limitation of milk intake to one glass a day

17. Tonya's mother tells you that she is upset because Tonya sometimes wets the bed. A urinalysis reveals no sig-nificant findings. After review of the pathophysiology of sickle cell and vaso-occlusive crisis with her, which of the following should you tell the mother?

a. To limit Tonya's fluids after dinner and especially at bedtime
b. To keep reminding Tonya that most girls her age do not wet the bed
c. To wake Tonya in the middle of the night and take her to the bathroom
d. To encourage Tonya to drink fluids and put a waterproof covering on her bed

18. Tonya's mother has brought her to the clinic because she has had fever of 101°F for the past 2 days and her appetite has been poor. Physical examination reveals no apparent cause for the fever. Appro-priate treatment includes:

a. Acetaminophen for fever and reevaluating Tonya in 24 hours
b. Ibuprofen for fever and reevalu-ating Tonya in 24 hours
c. Inpatient or outpatient antibiotic therapy
d. No treatment unless the fever is above 102°F

19. To prevent complications of sickle cell disease during the ages 3 months to 5 years, daily doses of which medication should be prescribed prophylactically?

    a. Baby aspirin
    b. Acetaminophen
    c. Diphenhydramine
    d. Penicillin

20. Mrs. S. has brought her toddler to the clinic for an immunization update. While talking to her, you learn that they live in an old building that has been under renovation for the past 2 months. Based on this information, you should first assess the child for:

    a. Asbestosis
    b. Coccidioidomycosis
    c. Mold allergy
    d. Lead poisoning

◘ ANSWERS AND RATIONALE

1. **(d)** Sulfa drugs precipitate hemolysis in patients with G6PD.

2. **(a)** Anorexia and irritability usually indicate some illness or abnormality and are common with anemia but are non-specific. Pallor is associated with anemia but may also be caused by familial skin color, limited exposure to sun, vasoconstriction, and fear. Asking the mother about April's diet prior to illness will help determine whether April was receiving enough iron in the diet and can help determine the differential diagnosis.

3. **(d)** An abnormality of more than one formed element of the blood (RBC, WBC, or platelets) may indicate aplastic anemia (bone marrow dysfunction) or cancer, and should be evaluated by a physician.

4. **(a)** In the first stage of iron deficiency, the body's iron stores are decreased. This can be detected by a fall in serum ferritin. No red blood cell changes are present in the first stage of iron deficiency because there is enough iron to support red blood cell formation.

5. **(d)** Iron deficiency anemia is the most likely diagnosis of anemia characterized by microcytosis (decreased MCV) and hypochromia (decreased MCH).

6. **(d)** The highest frequency of iron deficiency occurs during early childhood and adolescence, the same periods when growth is most rapid.

7. **(b)** Nutritional deficiency is the most common cause of iron deficiency anemia.

8. **(a)** About twice as much iron is absorbed on an empty stomach as at mealtime. Iron is given with meals only if gastric irritation or nausea is a problem.

9. **(c)** When the child is otherwise healthy, recovery from iron deficiency anemia is about two thirds complete in 1 month. Reevaluation of hemoglobin is recommended at 1 month. The mother should have already been taught about iron-rich foods, and the stool would be checked initially or, now, only if positive response to iron therapy was not seen.

10. **(d)** After hemoglobin levels have been restored, additional iron supplements are needed to replenish the body's iron stores.

11. **(d)** Because preterm infants have a smaller iron endowment and greater growth requirements after birth, oral iron supplements are recommended.

12. **(a)** Severe hypochromia and microcytosis as well as poikilocytes and target cells are seen in thalassemia. Poikilocytes and target cells do not characterize iron deficiency anemia. Pernicious anemia is macrocytic.

13. **(a)** Lead poisoning causes hypochromic, microcytic anemia. Pernicious anemia and folic acid deficiency are associated with macrocytosis.

14. **(a)** Iron deficiency caused by dietary deficiency is uncommon in the newborn. More common etiologies in this age are blood loss, hemolysis, and decreased red blood cell production.

15. **(d)** Sickle cell prep and Sickledex are screening tests and do not differentiate between sickle cell trait and sickle cell disease. Diagnosis is dependent on hemoglobin electrophoresis.

16. **(a)** Vaso-occlusive crisis is usually associated with infection, dehydration, acidosis, or exposure to cold. Many infections, especially respiratory, are largely spread by fomites than from hand to nose, or eye contact.

17. **(d)** Vaso-occlusive crisis is usually associated with infection, dehydration, acidosis, or exposure to cold. Hemodilution helps prevent vaso-occlusion. Fluids should always be encouraged, and bed wetting is common in young children who drink fluids near bedtime.

18. **(c)** If no simple cause is found for fever in patients with sickle cell disease, they should be treated as inpatients with IV antibiotics or outpatients with broad spectrum antibiotics.

19. **(d)** Antibiotic prophylaxis is given to the child with sickle cell disease from ages 3 months to 5 years to reduce the risk of infection and subsequent vaso-occlusive crisis.

20. **(d)** The main source of lead for children is dust in a house with deteriorated lead-based paint. Any house built before 1960 is suspect, and renovation will result in airborne dust mixed with lead. Mold allergy is common but not as serious as lead poisoning. Answers "a" and "b" are not as common in children compared to lead poisoning.

◘ REFERENCES

American Academy of Pediatrics. (2002). Health supervision for children with sickle cell disease. *Pediatrics, 109*, 3, 526–535.

American Academy of Pediatrics. (2004). Management of hyperbilirubinemia in the newborn infant 35 or more weeks of gestation. *Pediatrics, 114*, 1, 297–316.

American Academy of Pediatrics. (2009). *Red book online.* Available at: http://aapredbook.aappublications.org/. Accessed January 16, 2010.

Behrman, R. E., Kliegman, R. M., & Jensen, H. B. (Eds.). (2004). *Nelson textbook of pediatrics* (17th ed.). Philadelphia, PA: W. B. Saunders Company.

Centers for Disease Control and Prevention. (2002). *Managing elevated blood lead levels among young children: Recommendations from the Advisory Committee on Childhood Lead Poisoning Prevention.* Atlanta, GA: Author.

Custer, J. W., & Rau, R. E. (Eds.). (2009). *The Harriet Lane handbook* (18th ed.). St. Louis, MO: Mosby.

Hay, W. W., Haywood, A. R., Levin, M. J., & Sondheimer, J. M. (Eds.). (2009). *Current pediatric diagnosis & treatment* (19th ed.). Stamford, CT: McGraw-Hill/Appleton & Lange.

McMillan, J. A., Feigin, R. D., DeAngelis, C., & Jones, M. D. (Eds.). (2006). *Oski's pediatrics: Principles and practice.* (4th ed.). Philadelphia, PA: Lippincott Williams & Wilkins.

National Institutes of Health. (2002). *Management of sickle cell disease* (4th ed., NIH Publication No. 20–2117). Washington, DC: US Government Printing Office.

Newman, T. B., Kuzniewicz, M. W, Liljestrand, P., Wi, S., McCulloch, C., & Escobar, G. J. (2009). Numbers needed to treat with phototherapy according to American Academy of Pediatrics guidelines. *Pediatrics, 123*, 5, 1352–1359.

Yetman, R. J. (2003). Evaluation and management of childhood idiopathic (immune) thrombocytopenia. *Journal of Pediatric Health Care, 17*, 261–263.

Endocrine Disorders

Malinda D. Duke

Select one best answer to the following questions.

1. You receive the results of newborn screening and find that the TSH, done at day 2, is 82. What is your best option?

   a. Have the child come to the clinic next week for a reevaluation.
   b. Rescreen the child in one month.
   c. Begin thyroid supplementation immediately.
   d. Reassure the family that these are normal results.

2. You are evaluating a 13-year-old girl for Graves' disease. Which of the following signs would not support this diagnosis?

   a. An enlarged thyroid
   b. Exophthalmos
   c. A positive family history
   d. An elevated TSH level

3. The routine screening of a newborn in your practice indicates that the baby has congenital hypothyroidism and is in need of a referral to a pediatric endocrinologist. The treatment of choice for congenital or acquired hypothyroidism is:

   a. Levothyroxine
   b. Propylthiouracil
   c. Potassium iodide
   d. Radiation therapy

4. A child in your clinic is being evaluated for short stature. Pertinent findings include delayed bone age, delayed onset of puberty, and a stature that is normal for the child's bone age. In addition, the mother states that the child's father grew taller in college and wonders if this will happen with their son. The most likely cause of these findings is:

   a. Familial short stature
   b. Chromosomal abnormality
   c. Constitutional delay of growth and puberty
   d. Endocrine abnormality

5. Which chromosomal abnormality is associated with short stature in girls?

   a. Down syndrome
   b. Turner syndrome
   c. Klinefelter's syndrome
   d. Prader-Willi syndrome

6. Achondroplasia refers to a growth delay that is:

    a. Due to malabsorption
    b. Associated with Noonan syndrome
    c. Associated with endocrine disorders
    d. Manifested by disproportionately short stature

7. You are following a 4-year-old girl in your practice with a history of breast development that appeared 12 months ago and appears to be progressing. She is growing rapidly. The PNP considers ordering a bone age because she knows that most cases of premature thelarche in girls are:

    a. A result of enzymatic defects
    b. Due to systemic CNS disease
    c. Idiopathic
    d. A result of hypothyroidism

8. The mother of an 11-year-old boy is concerned that her son is developing secondary sexual characteristics too early. Your counseling for this family is based on the knowledge that puberty is considered precocious in boys if secondary sexual characteristics appear prior to age:

    a. 12
    b. 11
    c. 10
    d. 9

9. Treatment of true (central) precocious puberty is best achieved with:

    a. Synthetic follicular stimulating hormone
    b. Gonadotropin releasing hormone
    c. Dexamethasone
    d. Thyroid hormone

10. The pathophysiology of type 1 diabetes is:

    a. Autoimmune destruction of the pancreatic beta cells
    b. Primary insulin receptor resistance
    c. Increased hepatic glucose production
    d. Reduced glucose uptake by target tissue

11. An 11-year-old girl presents at a well-child visit with symptoms of polyuria and polydipsia. Which of the following diagnoses must be ruled out?

    a. Diabetes mellitus
    b. Hyperthyroidism
    c. Adrenocortical insufficiency
    d. Nephrotic syndrome

12. For children with diabetes, in addition to home monitoring of blood glucose and urine ketone levels, glycosylated hemoglobin (Hgb A_{1c}) should be measured every:

    a. 1 week
    b. 1 month
    c. 3 months
    d. 6 months

13. Mrs. W. has brought her 1-year-old baby to the clinic for a well-baby examination. She is pregnant with her second child and is concerned about possible risks to the fetus because she has gestational class A diabetes. Which of the following conditions is the fetus not at risk for?

    a. Congenital anomalies
    b. Hypoglycemia
    c. Birth trauma
    d. Congenital hearing loss

14. Infants with IUGR are prone to hypoglycemia primarily because they:

    a. Have a decreased metabolic rate
    b. Have little glucose stores in the form of glycogen and fat
    c. Become acidotic
    d. Are prone to sepsis

15. During the first well-baby visit of Joshua, 2 weeks old, his mother says that she is concerned because his penis looks different from his 3-year-old brother's penis. During the physical exam, you notice that the baby's scrotum is hyperpigmented. The PNP knows that the most common cause of ambiguous genitalia is:

    a. Idiopathic
    b. A chromosomal defect
    c. Congenital adrenal hyperplasia (CAH)
    d. An embryologic disorder

16. Which of the following signs or symptoms is not associated with congenital adrenal hyperplasia:

    a. Hypernatremia
    b. Progressive weight loss
    c. Dehydration
    d. Hyperkalemia

17. Families of children with congenital adrenal hyperplasia must be educated about:

    a. The self-limiting aspect of the disorder
    b. The need for genetic counseling
    c. Dietary restrictions
    d. The need for strict replacement therapy

18. The mother of a 14-year-old girl indicates to you that she is concerned because the girl has not yet started to menstruate. The history is noncontributory and the physical examination is normal. Breast development and pubic hair have been present for 12 months. The most appropriate initial step would be to:

    a. Do a pregnancy test
    b. Obtain a buccal smear for chromosomal analysis
    c. Reassure, educate the family, and follow-up
    d. Draw LH and FSH levels

19. Primary dysmenorrhea is due to:

    a. Elevated prostaglandin level
    b. Pelvic inflammatory disease (PID)
    c. Endometriosis
    d. Fibroids

20. The differential diagnosis of dysfunctional uterine bleeding includes all but which of the following?

    a. Pregnancy-related disorders
    b. Anemia
    c. Foreign body
    d. Endometriosis

21. An 11-month-old African American boy has just started walking and is found to have severely bowed legs. In the history, you learn that he is exclusively breastfed with very little other food intake. You must consider:

    a. Trauma
    b. Developmental variation
    c. Chromosomal abnormality
    d. Rickets

◘ ANSWERS AND RATIONALE

1. **(c)** Congenital thyroid screening is done prior to discharge and before day 7 of life by measuring T_4 and TSH. If the T_4 is >6.5 μg/dl and the TSH is >20 μU/ml, the infant should be started immediately on thyroid replacement and referred to a pediatric endocrinologist.

2. **(d)** In hyperthyroidism, the TSH level, which is under negative feedback control by the pituitary gland, is suppressed.

3. **(a)** Levothyroxine is the drug of choice for treating hypothyroidism. Choices "b," "c," and "d" are treatments for hyperthyroidism.

4. **(c)** Constitutional delay is characterized by a bone age that is delayed for chronologic age and a normal growth velocity for bone age. If the growth velocity was decreasing, you must consider a growth deficiency and refer to endocrinology.

5. **(b)** Turner syndrome, which occurs in girls, is associated with stature below the third percentile in 99% of affected cases.

6. **(d)** Achondroplasia, or skeletal dysplasia, is an autosomal dominant mutation that results in disproportionate short stature (e.g., shortened limbs, macrocephaly, and bowing of legs). It is not responsive to growth hormone therapy.

7. **(c)** Sexual precocity is idiopathic in 80% of girls. The PNP, however, should refer the child to pediatric endocrine to

evaluate for advancing bone age and progressive clinical signs since some children require treatment.

8. **(d)** Precocious puberty is defined as secondary sex characteristics appearing before age 9 in boys and age 8 in girls.

9. **(b)** Central precocious puberty is suppressible with analogues of long-acting gonadotropin-releasing hormone (GnRH).

10. **(a)** Type 1 diabetes is an autoimmune disease in which islet cell antibodies destroy the pancreatic beta cells. The other causes of hyperglycemia are seen in type 2 diabetes.

11. **(a)** Essential signs of diabetes mellitus include polyuria, polydipsia, weight loss, hyperglycemia, and glucosuria. Nephrotic syndrome may present following an influenza-like episode with periorbital swelling and oliguria.

12. **(c)** HgbA$_{1c}$ should be measured every 3 months. This test reflects a weighted mean of the frequency of elevated blood glucose levels over the previous 3 months, with greatest influence in the previous month.

13. **(d)** The infant of a mother with gestational diabetes is often macrosomic and also at increased risk for trauma, congenital anomalies, and hypoglycemia.

14. **(b)** IUGR infants have reduced glucose stores in the form of glycogen and body fat, and therefore are prone to hypoglycemia.

15. **(c)** CAH is the most common cause of ambiguous genitalia.

16. **(a)** Hyponatremia (not hypernatremia) is a sign of CAH as there is excessive sodium loss through the kidneys and an inability to maintain serum electrolyte balance.

17. **(d)** Families should be counseled about the need for lifelong medication therapy and follow-up. They will also need to understand "stress" dosing (injectable form) for fevers of greater than 101°F degrees, trauma, surgery, and persistent vomiting.

18. **(c)** Primary amenorrhea is defined by absence of menarche by 16 years of age with normal pubertal growth, and development or absence of menarche 2 years after sexual maturation is completed. After age 16, referral to endocrinology might be indicated. It is relatively uncommon and often due to constitutional delay.

19. **(a)** Primary dysmenorrhea is due to an excessive production of uterine prostaglandins causing uterine hypercontractility, tissue ischemia, and nerve hypersensitivity. The other causes may lead to secondary dysmenorrhea.

20. **(b)** Anemia is considered to be a complication of dysfunctional uterine bleeding rather than a part of the differential diagnosis.

21. **(d)** Rickets is often connected to nutrition. By 11 months of age, babies need a wide variety of foods. Additionally, breastmilk in African American mothers is lower in vitamin D concentrations than breastmilk from mothers of other ethnicities.

◻ REFERENCES

Alemzadeh, R., Rising, R., & Lifshitz, F. (2007). In F. Lifshitz (Ed.), *Pediatric endocrinology* (5th ed., Vol. 1, pp. 1–56). New York, NY: Informa Healthcare USA Inc.

Carrillo, A. A., & Bao, Y. (2007). Hormonal dynamic tests and genetic tests used in pediatric endocrinology. In F. Lifshitz (Ed.), *Pediatric endocrinology* (5th ed., Vol. 2, pp. 737–767). New York, NY: Informa Healthcare USA Inc.

Chase, H. P. (2006). *Understanding diabetes* (11th ed.). Denver, CO: Barbara Davis Center for Childhood Diabetes.

Cooke, D. W., & Plotnick, L. (2008). Type 1 diabetes mellitus in pediatrics. *Pediatrics in Review, 29,* 11, 374–385.

Crimmins, N. A., & Dolan, L. M. (2008). Definition, diagnosis, and classification of diabetes in youth. In D. Dabelea, & G. J. Klingensmith, (Eds.) *Epidemiology of pediatric and adolescent diabetes* (pp. 1–19). New York, NY: Informa Healthcare USA Inc.

Dallas, J. S. (2007). Hyperthyroidism. In F. Lifshitz (Ed.), *Pediatric endocrinology* (5th ed., Vol. 2, pp. 391–404). New York, NY: Informa Healthcare USA Inc.

Farrag, H. M., & Cowett, R. M. (2007). Hypoglycemia in the newborn. In F. Lifshitz (Ed.), *Pediatric endocrinology* (5th ed., Vol. 2, pp. 330–358). New York, NY: Informa Healthcare USA Inc.

Fleishman, A., & Gordon, C. (2007). Adolescent menstrual abnormalities. In F. Lifshitz (Ed.), *Pediatric endocrinology* (5th ed., Vol. 2, pp. 349–363). New York, NY: Informa Healthcare USA Inc.

Garber, J. R., & Koury, C. B. (2009). Treatment of hyper- and hypothyroidism. *Review of Endocrinology, 3,* 4, 20–22.

Gharib, H., & Koury, C. B. (2009). Diagnosis and management of thyroid nodules: An overview. *Review of Endocrinology, 3,* 4, 23–25.

Grimberg, A., & De Leon, D. D. (2005). Disorders of growth. In T. Moshang (Ed.), *Pediatric endocrinology: The requisites in pediatrics* (pp. 127–167). St. Louis, MO: Mosby.

Grimberg, A., & Lifshitz, F. (2008). Worrisome growth. In M. Sperling (Ed.), *Pediatric endocrinology* (3rd ed., pp. 1–50). Philadelphia, PA: Saunders.

Halac, I., & Zimmerman, D. (2004). Evaluating short stature in children. *Pediatric Annals, 33,* 3, 170–176.

Henry, J. J. (2004). *Cortisol replacement therapy: An educational booklet for parents and children* (2nd ed.). Gaithersburg, MD: Pediatric Endocrinology Nursing Society.

Henwood, M. J., & Levitt Katz, L. E. (2005). Disorders of the adrenal gland. In T. Moshang (Ed.), *Pediatric endocrinology: The requisites in pediatrics,* (pp. 193–213). St. Louis, MO: Mosby.

Huang, S. A. (2007). Hypothyroidism. In F. Lifshitz (Ed.), *Pediatric endocrinology* (5th ed., Vol. 2, pp. 391–404). New York, NY: Informa Healthcare USA Inc.

Huang, S. A. (2007). Thyromegly. In F. Lifshitz (Ed.), *Pediatric endocrinology* (5th ed., Vol. 2, pp. 443–453). New York, NY: Informa Healthcare USA Inc.

Hubbard, V. S. (2000). Defining overweight and obesity: What are the issues? *American Journal Clinical Nursing, 72,* 5, 1067–1068.

Kache, S., & Ferry, R. J., Jr. (2005). Diabetes insipidus. In T. Moshang (Ed.), *Pediatric endocrinology: The requisites in pediatrics* (pp. 257–267). St. Louis, MO: Mosby.

Kappy, M. S., Steelman, J. W., Travers, S. H., & Zeitler, P. S. (2003). Endocrine Disorders. In W. W. Hay, Jr., A. R. Hayward, M. J. Levin, & J. M. Sondheimer (Eds.), *Current pediatric diagnosis and treatment* (16th ed., pp. 937–977). New York, NY: Lange Medical/McGraw-Hill.

Lee, P. A. (2005). Early pubertal development. In T. Moshang (Ed.), *Pediatric endocrinology: The requisites in pediatrics* (pp. 73–86). St. Louis, MO: Mosby.

Lee, P. A., & Houk, C. P. (2007). Puberty and its disorders. In F. Lifshitz (Ed.), Pediatric endocrinology (5th ed., Vol. 2, pp. 273–324). New York, NY: Informa Healthcare USA Inc.

Lee, P. A., & Kulin, H. E. (2005). Normal pubertal development. In T. Moshang (Ed.) *Pediatric endocrinology: The requisites in pediatrics* (pp. 63–72). St. Louis, MO: Mosby.

Loscalzo, M. L. (2008). Turner Syndrome. *Pediatrics in Review, 29,* 7, 219–226.

Lustig, R. H., & Weiss, R. (2008). In M. Sperling (Ed.), *Pediatric endocrinology* (3rd ed., pp. 788–838), Philadelphia, PA: Saunders.

Lyles, S. P., Silverstein, J. H., & Rosenbloom, A. L. (2007). Practical aspects of diabetes care. In F. Lifshitz (Ed.), *Pediatric endocrinology* (5th ed., Vol. 1, pp. 125–154). New York, NY: Informa Healthcare USA Inc.

Mahoney, C. P. (1990). Adolescent gynecomastia: Differential diagnosis and management. *Pediatric Clinics of North America, 37,* 6, 1389–1404.

Migeon, C. J., & Lanes, R. (2007). Adrenal cortex: Hypo- and hyperfunction. In F. Lifshitz (Ed.), *Pediatric endocrinology* (5th ed., Vol. 2, pp. 195–229). New York, NY: Informa Healthcare USA Inc.

Miller, W. L., Achermann, J. C., & Fluck, C. E. (2008). The adrenal cortex and its disorders. In M. Sperling (Ed.), *Pediatric endocrinology* (3rd ed., pp. 444–511), Philadelphia, PA: Saunders.

Muglia, L. J., & Majzoub, J. A. (2008). Disorders of the posterior pituitary. In M. Sperling (Ed.), *Pediatric endocrinology* (3rd ed., pp. 335–373), Philadelphia, PA: Saunders.

Muir, A. (2006). Precocious puberty. *Pediatrics in Review, 27*, 10, 373–381.

New, M. I., Ghizzoni, L., & Lin-Su, K. (2007). An update of congenital adrenal hyperplasia. In F. Lifshitz (Ed.), *Pediatric endocrinology* (5th ed., Vol. 2, pp. 227–245). New York, NY: Informa Healthcare USA Inc.

Raine, J. E., Donaldson, M. D., Gregory, J. W., Savage, M. O., & Hintz, R. L. (Eds.), (2006). *Practical endocrinology and diabetes in children* (2nd ed., pp. 91–108). Malden, MA: Blackwell Publishing Ltd.

Rosenbloom, A. L. & Connor, E. L. (2007). Hypopituitarism and other disorders of the growth hormone-insulin-like growth factor-1 axis. In F. Lifshitz (Ed.), *Pediatric endocrinology* (5th ed., Vol. 2, pp. 65–99). New York, NY: Informa Healthcare USA Inc.

Rosenfeld, R .G., & Cohen, P. (2008). Disorders of growth hormone/insulin-like growth factor secretion and action. In M. Sperling (Ed.), *Pediatric endocrinology* (3rd ed., pp. 254–334), Philadelphia, PA: Saunders.

Rosenfield, R. L., Cooke, D. W., & Radovick, S. (2008). Puberty and its disorders in the female. In M. Sperling (Ed.), *Pediatric endocrinology* (3rd ed., pp. 530–609). Philadelphia, PA: Saunders.

Rossi, W. C., Caplin, N., & Alter, C. A. (2005). Thyroid disorders in children. In T. Moshang (Ed.), *Pediatric endocrinology: The requisites in pediatrics* (pp. 171–190). St. Louis, MO: Mosby.

Shomaker, K., Bradford, K., & Key-Solle, M. (2009). The infant with ambiguous genitalia: The pediatrician's role. *Contemporary pediatrics, 26*, 4, 40–56.

Thorton, P. S. (2005). Thyroid disorders in children. In T. Moshang (Ed.), *Pediatric endocrinology: The requisites in pediatrics* (pp. 37–59). St. Louis, MO: Mosby.

Van Vliet, G., & Polack, M. (2007). Thyroid disorders in infancy. In F. Lifshitz (Ed.), *Pediatric endocrinology* (5th ed., Vol. 2, pp. 391–404). New York, NY: Informa Healthcare USA Inc.

Winter, W. E. (2007). Autoimmune endocrinopathies. In F. Lifshitz (Ed.), *Pediatric endocrinology* (5th ed., Vol. 2, pp. 595–616). New York, NY: Informa Healthcare USA Inc.

◘ EDUCATIONAL WEB SITES

www.caresfoundation.org (Congenital Adrenal Hyperplasia)

www.childrenwithdiabetes.com (Pediatric Diabetes)

www.diabetes.org (American Diabetes Association—all diabetes)

www.diabetes.org/schooltraining (ADA's training curriculum for schools)

www.dsdguidelines.org/files/clinical.pdf (Intersex Society of North America "Scripts for talking with parents")

www.hgfound.org (Human Growth Foundation)

www.hormone.org

www.jdrf.org (Juvenile Diabetes Research Foundation)

www.magicfoundation.org (all endocrine disorders)

www.pens.org (Pediatric Endocrinology Nursing Society)

www.pituitary.org

14

Multisystem and Genetic Disorders

Rita Marie John

Select one best answer to the following questions.

1. A 2-month-old child presents after an episode of sepsis for a follow-up visit. He has gained 2 lbs since birth and has a decrease in head circumference from the 50th to the 25th percentile. In addition, he has inguinal and axillary adenopathy of 1 cm, decrease in head, and has hepatomegaly. Which of the following is included in the infectious disease differential?

   a. Herpes simplex type 2 infection
   b. Human immunodeficiency virus infection
   c. Chlamydia infection
   d. Congenital gonorrhea

2. Which of the following is the most helpful in confirming a diagnosis of *Chlamydia pneumoniae* in a 1-month-old child with a cough?

   a. Chest x-ray showing lobar consolidation
   b. Decrease serum immunoglobulins
   c. Lymphocytosis
   d. Mother with no prenatal care

3. A social worker brings a child in prior to placement with a chief complaint of copious vaginal discharge. A culture is positive for *Chlamydia*. From the social perspective, what is the next best step?

   a. Reassure the social worker that this is a prenatal transmission.
   b. Tell the social worker the result and allow her to decide the next step.
   c. Tell the social worker the result and inform her of the likelihood of sexual abuse.
   d. Call the foster family with the result.

4. Which of the following is a nontreponemal test for syphilis?

   a. Venereal Disease Research Laboratory (VDRL) microscopic slide test
   b. Fluorescent treponemal antibody absorbed (FTA-ABS)
   c. *Treponema pallidum* particle agglutination (TP-PA)
   d. TORCH titer

5. Which anticipatory guidance would be helpful in decreasing the risk of toxoplasmosis?

   a. When camping, treat water from streams with iodine.
   b. Do not go barefoot in high-risk areas.
   c. Wash hands after changing cat litter.
   d. Avoid handling contaminated diapers.

6. What physical exam finding distinguishes a newborn with congenital toxoplasmosis from a newborn with congenital cytomegalovirus (CMV)?

   a. Jaundice
   b. Microcephaly
   c. Cerebral calcifications
   d. Petechial rash

7. What congenital infection can present with snuffles, lymphadenopathy, pseudoparalysis of Parrot, CNS abnormalities, and low birth weight?

   a. Cytomegalovirus
   b. Rubella
   c. Toxoplasmosis
   d. Syphilis

8. A child presents with a flattened philtrum, thin upper lip, micrognathia, strabismus, and a ventricular septal defect. What is the most likely diagnosis?

   a. Congenital toxoplasmosis
   b. Congenital syphilis
   c. Fetal alcohol syndrome
   d. Edwards syndrome

9. A five-year-old girl presents for a school physical with a complaint of hyperactivity, a mild developmental delay, aversion of gaze, hand mannerism, and long thin face with a slightly dysmorphic ear. What is the most likely diagnosis?

   a. Fragile X
   b. Turner's syndrome
   c. Fetal alcohol syndrome
   d. William's syndrome

10. Which of the following physical exam findings is a major criterion for identifying a patient with Marfan syndrome?

    a. Brushfield spots
    b. Shield chest with widely spaced nipples
    c. Pectus excavatum requiring surgery
    d. Large testicles

11. Which of the following is found more commonly in children with a meningomyelocele?

    a. Congenital heart disease
    b. Latex allergy
    c. Intestinal malformations
    d. Cleft palate

12. A 2-year-old girl has lymphedema of the hands and foot, with low posterior hairline, cubitus valgus, and a history of intrauterine growth retardation. Which of the following defects is most common among the children with this genetic syndrome?

    a. Aortic valve stenosis
    b. Coarctation of the aorta
    c. Mitral valve prolapse
    d. Dissecting aortic aneurysm

13. Which of the following screenings is done annually on a 4-year-old child with Down syndrome?

    a. Cervical spine
    b. Urinalysis
    c. Celiac screening
    d. Thyroid screening

14. A 6-year-old child has +4 reflexes, toe walking, and a clumsy gait. Which of the following diagnostic testing would be the helpful in making a diagnosis of cerebral palsy?

    a. Skull x-ray
    b. Computerized tomography of the head
    c. Magnetic resonance imaging of the head
    d. Magnetic resonance imaging of the lumbosacral spine

15. What hormone needs replacement in adolescents with Klinefelter's syndrome?

    a. Thyroid hormone
    b. Growth hormone
    c. Estrogen
    d. Testosterone

16. A 9-month-old child of Jewish parents presents with increasing irritability and noise sensitivity. What is the next best step?

    a. Encourage mom to decrease environmental stimuli
    b. Refer to a pediatrician
    c. Refer for further developmental screening
    d. Reevaluate at the 12-month examination

17. A newborn presents with microcephaly, low-set ears, prominent occiput, micrognathia, heart murmur, and clenched hands with overriding fingers and crossed thumb. What is best diagnostic test?

    a. Karyotype
    b. Amino acid urine screen
    c. Newborn screening
    d. Methylation test

18. A 2.5-year-old child presents with a macrocephaly, developmental delay, coarse facial features, large tongue, kyphosis, hip dislocation, tonsillar and adenoidal hypertrophy, and hepatomegaly. She is receiving early intervention services without improvement. What is the next best step?

    a. Referral to genetics for further evaluation
    b. Follow up in 3 months
    c. Reassure the parents
    d. Follow up in 6 months

◻ ANSWERS AND RATIONALE

1. **(b)** Human immunodeficiency virus can present with lymphadenopathy, poor weight gain, decreased head circumference, and serious bacterial infections.

2. **(d)** A chest x-ray of a child will show hyperinflation rather than lobar infiltrates. The child with chlamydia will have elevated immunoglobulins and peripheral eosinophilia. The lack of prenatal care is a risk factor for chlamydia pneumonitis.

3. **(c)** The child with an active chlamydia infection after age 18 months is a victim of childhood sexual assault. This infection needs to be treated, but the social worker needs to be aware of the implication of a positive result.

4. **(a)** There are nontreponemal tests such as Venereal Disease Research Laboratory (VDRL) microscopic slide test and rapid plasma reagin (RPR), which are initial screening tests. Usually, a nontreponemal test is performed first and if it is reactive then a treponemal test is done. The fluorescent treponemal antibody absorbed is the most treponemal test used to confirm a positive RPR. The FTA-ABS remains positive and becomes reactive earlier. Since it remains positive after treatment, the test does not indicate current disease state or the need for treatment. The other treponemal test used to confirm a nontreponemal test include a *Treponema pallidum* particle agglutination (TP-PA).

5. **(c)** Transmission of toxoplasmosis occurs through handling of cat feces. Pregnant women should avoid contact with cat litter, and others should wash hands thoroughly when handling cat litter.

6. **(d)** A petechial rash is common in cytomegalovirus but rare in toxoplasmosis. Jaundice may be seen in both conditions. Cerebral calcifications may also be found in both conditions. Microcephaly, which may appear at birth or manifest within a few months, is likewise seen in both CMV and toxoplasmosis.

7. **(d)** The classic presentation of congenitally acquired syphilis includes low birth weight/prematurity; rhinitis (snuffles); mucous patches; jaundice with elevated liver enzymes; lymphadenopathy with Coombs-negative hemolytic anemia; osteochondritis, which causes resistance to movement (pseudoparalysis of Parrot); CNS abnormalities; and a rash similar to secondary syphilis with desquamation of hands and feet (Hyman & Adam, 2006; AAP, 2009). The presentation of toxoplasmosis includes microcephaly, seizures, maculopapular rash, hepatosplenomegaly, and jaundice.

8. **(c)** Fetal alcohol spectrum disorders include fetal alcohol syndrome, alcohol-related neurodevelopmental disorder (ARND), and alcohol-related birth defects (ARBD). The physical findings of fetal alcohol syndrome includes all of the physical findings listed. It can also include wide-spaced eyes with narrow lids and epicanthal folds, seizure disorder, microcephaly, dental malocclusion, hearing and vision impairment, growth impairment, cleft palate, and attention deficit disorder.

9. **(a)** Children with fragile X have some similar behavioral characteristics as patients with autism spectrum disorder. The characteristics of hyperactivity, a mild developmental delay, aversion of gaze, hand mannerism, and a long thin face with large ears is consistent with fragile X. Females with Turner's syndrome have short stature without distinctive behavioral characteristics.

10. **(c)** White speckling of the iris is referred to as Brushfield spots, which is associated with trisomy 21 syndrome (Down syndrome), but may also be a normal variant. A shield chest with wide-spaced nipples is associated with Turner's syndrome. Large testicles are associated with fragile X. However, pectus excavatum requiring surgery is a major skeletal criteria.

11. **(b)** The associated problems of children with myelodysplasia include neurologic problems such as hydrocephalus, seizures, skin breakdowns, cognitive deficits, and learning issues. Other problems are bowel and bladder problems, visual problems, and musculoskeletal deformities. Allergic reactions to latex are common with up to 73% having latex allergies. Cardiac defects, intestinal malformations, and cleft palate are not major problems for children with myelodysplasias.

12. **(b)** Coarctation of the aorta with or without a bicuspid aortic valve is the most commonly cardiac problem associated with Turner's syndrome.

13. **(d)** Children with Down syndrome are at greater risk for thyroid disease and leukemia. The guidelines from the American Academy of Pediatrics recommend a thyroid screening yearly by objective laboratory testing at birth, at 6 months, and yearly thereafter. Atlantoaxial dislocation can be screened for at 3 years of age. Celiac disease can be found in up to 5 to 12% of patients affected by Down syndrome.

14. **(c)** MRI of the brain is the most helpful in children with suspected CP and about 90% will show some abnormalities including major and minor brain malformation, strokes, and white matter loss.

15. **(d)** Males with Klinefelter's syndrome need testosterone due to inadequate virilization. The thyroid is not usually affected.

16. **(b)** Tay-Sachs's disease is seen in families of Ashkenazi Jewish descent and

is characterized by degenerative CNS signs and hyperreaction to noise. A consultation with the pediatrician is indicated due to the possibility of Tay-Sach's disease.

17. **(a)** Individuals with Edwards syndrome have trisomy of chromosome 18, which can be evaluated with a karyotype. A newborn screening will look for biochemical, hemoglobin, thyroid, and metabolic disorders. Amino acid screening will specifically evaluate for amino acid deficiencies or excesses but would not be helpful in this case. In doing methylation tests, there is PCR amplification of individual DNA fragments. These tests are done to rule out such genetic disorders as Prader-Willi syndrome and Angelman syndrome.

18. **(a)** This child has many of the signs of Hurler's syndrome. Given the lack of progress in early intervention and the physical assessment findings, a referral to genetics would be the best approach in this child.

◘ REFERENCES

Atkinson, W., Wolfe, S., Hamborsky, J., & McIntyre, L. (Eds.). (2009). *Epidemiology and prevention of vaccine-preventable diseases* (11th ed.). Washington, DC: Centers for Disease Control and Prevention

American Academy of Pediatrics. (2009). Section 1, Active and passive immunizations and Section 2, Recommendations for care of children in special circumstances. In L. K. Pickering (Ed.), *Red book 2009: Report of the committee on infectious diseases* (28th ed.). Elk Grove Village, IL: Author.

American Academy of Pediatrics and the Committee on Genetics. (2007). *Health supervision for children with Down syndrome.* Available at: http://aappolicy.aappublications .org/cgi/content/full/pediatrics;107/2/442. Accessed July 1, 2009.

Betrand, J., Floyd, R., & Weber, M. (2005). Guidelines for identifying and referring persons with fetal alcohol syndrome. *Morbidity and Mortality Weekly Reports, 54*, RR11, 1–10

Bondy, C. (2007). Care of girls and women with Turner syndrome: A guideline of the Turner syndrome study group. *The Journal of Clinical Endocrinology & Metabolism, 92*, 1, 10–25.

Centers for Disease Control and Prevention. (2009). *Cytomegalovirus.* Available at: http:// www.cdc.gov/Features/dsCytomegalovirus/. Accessed June 30, 2009.

Chandran, L., & Boykan, R. (2009). Chlamydial infections in children and adolescents. *Pediatrics in Review, 30*, 243–250.

Committee on Genetics. (2007). Health supervision for children with Marfan syndrome. *Pediatrics, 120*, 3, 683–684.

Davidson, M. (2008). Primary care for children and adolescents with Down syndrome. *Pediatric Clinics of North America, 55*, 1099–1111.

Denny, C. H., Tsai, J., Floyd, R. L., & Green, P. P. (2009). Alcohol use among pregnant and nonpregnant women of childbearing age— United States, 1991–2005. *Morbidity and Mortality Weekly Report, 58*, 19, 529–532.

Dodge, N. (2008). Cerebral palsy: Medical aspects. *Pediatric Clinics of North America, 55*, 1189–1207.

Enright, A., & Prober, C. (2004). Herpesviridae infections in newborns: Varicella zoster virus, herpes simplex virus, and cytomegalovirus. *Pediatric Clinics of North America, 51*, 889–908.

Hagerman, R., Berry-Kravis, E., Kaufman, W. E., Ono, M., Tartaglia, N., Lachiewicz, A., *et al.* (2009). Advances in the treatment of fragile X syndrome. *Pediatrics, 123*, 1, 378–387.

Havens, P. L., Mofenson, L. M., & the Committee on Pediatric AIDS. (2009). Evaluation and management of the infant exposed to HIV-1 in the United States. *Pediatrics, 123*, 175–187.

Hill, I. D., Dirks, M. H., Liptak, G. S., Colletti, R. B., Fasano, A., Guandalini, S., *et al.* (2005). Guideline for the diagnosis and treatment for celiac disease in children: Recommendations of the North American Society for Pediatric Gastroenterology, Hepatology and Nutrition. *Journal of Pediatric Gastroenterology and Nutrition, 40*, 1, 1–19.

Hyman, E., & Adam, H. (2006). Syphilis. *Pediatrics in Review, 27,* 37–39.

Lazzaretti, C., & Pearson, C. (2009). In P. Allen, J. Vessey, & N. Schapiro (Eds.), *Primary care of the child with a chronic condition* (5th ed., pp. 671–685). St. Louis, MO: Mosby.

Muenzer, J., Wraith, J. E., & Clarke, L. A., & the International Consensus Panel on the Management and Treatment of Mucopolysaccharidosis I. (2009). Mucopolysaccharidosis I: Management and treatment guidelines. *Pediatrics, 123,* 1, 19–30.

Norton, M. E. (2008). Genetic screening and counseling. *Current Opinion in Pediatrics, 20,* 2, 157–163.

Paduch, D. A., Fine, R. G., Bolyakov, A., & Kiper, J. (2008). New concepts in Klinefelter syndrome. *Current Opinion in Urology, 18,* 6, 621–627.

Tamma, P., & Serwint, J. R. (2007). Toxoplasmosis. *Pediatrics in Review, 28,* 470–471.

15

Health Policy and Professional Issues

Janet Selway

Select one best answer to the following questions.

1. Which of the following is true with regard to advanced practice licensure?

   a. It is granted by some states based on specialty certification.
   b. It will guarantee reimbursement.
   c. It may be obtained on a national basis.
   d. It is a federal process verifying that a PNP has met standards for specialty practice.

2. A PNP may obtain certification from the PNCB and which other association?

   a. American College of Nurse Practitioners
   b. American Academy of Nurse Practitioners
   c. American Nurses Credentialing Center
   d. American Nurses Association

3. According to the Consensus Model for APRN Regulation, which of the following is most consistent with the definition of Advanced Practice Registered Nursing?

   a. Optional national certification
   b. A significant component of education and practice focuses on direct care of individuals
   c. Accountability excludes prescription of pharmacologic and nonpharmacologic intervention
   d. Level of role autonomy is unchanged

4. The granting of authority to practice is known as:

   a. Credentialing
   b. Accreditation
   c. Licensure
   d. Regulation

5. Payment by capitation means that:

   a. Financial risk is shifted from payers to providers
   b. Care is provided on a fee-for-service basis
   c. Care resources are rationed
   d. Target populations have unlimited access to health care

6. Which of the following is the purpose of certification?

   a. To review and approve educational degree programs in nursing
   b. To assure the public that an individual has mastered a body of knowledge and acquired skills in a particular body of knowledge
   c. All of the above
   d. None of the above

7. The mobilization, monitoring, and control of resources used by a patient over the course of an illness is called:

   a. Case management
   b. Quality improvement
   c. Quality assurance
   d. Risk management

8. Managed care plans may be certified by which of the following?

   a. Centers for Medicare and Medicaid Services (CMS)
   b. Department of Health and Human Services (DHHS)
   c. National Institutes of Health (NIH)
   d. National Committee for Quality Assurance (NCQA)

9. Prescriptive writing privileges:

   a. Require a formal collaborative relationship with a physician
   b. Are regulated by both boards of nursing and medicine
   c. Vary according to state statutes
   d. Are granted upon certification

10. Systematically developed statements to assist practitioner and patient about appropriate care for specific clinical outcomes are called:

    a. Clinical practice guidelines
    b. Benchmarking
    c. Protocol Requirements
    d. Written Collaborative Agreement

11. A main goal of continuous quality improvement is to:

    a. Incorporate norms, criteria, and standards as evaluative measures
    b. Emphasize outcome measures in addition to structure and process
    c. Promote evaluation based on peer review, audits, and chart reviews
    d. Inform that quality assurance is more than a periodic evaluation of performance

12. In documenting quality care, patient satisfaction is considered to be what type of measure?

    a. Structural
    b. Process
    c. Outcome
    d. Cost containment

13. Political activism through lobbying is an example of what type of change strategy?

    a. Normative reeducative
    b. Empirical rational
    c. Power-coercive
    d. Confrontational

14. The Early and Periodic Screening, Diagnostic, and Treatment (EPSDT) program describes a comprehensive set of healthcare services as provided by:

    a. Private insurance
    b. State child protection teams
    c. Medicaid
    d. Most managed care organizations

15. Scope of practice statements:

    a. Are prepared by national professional organizations
    b. Provide the basis for reimbursement policies
    c. Are written by employers
    d. May vary from state to state

◻ ANSWERS AND RATIONALE

1. **(a)** Licensure for advanced practice is available in many states if the applicant has demonstrated specialty certification.

2. **(c)** The American Nurses Credentialing Center (ANCC) and the Pediatric Nursing Certification Board (PNCB) are certifying bodies for a PNP.

3. **(b)** In the APRN Consensus Model for Future Regulation, seven characteristics of advanced practice registered nursing are described including: "the defining factor for all APRNs is that a significant component of the education and practice focuses on direct care of individuals" (APRN Consensus Workgroup, 2008, p. 6).

4. **(c)** "Licensure is the process by which an agency of state government grants authority to an individual to engage in a given profession upon finding that the applicant has attained the essential degree of competency necessary to perform a unique scope of practice." (NCSBN, 2010)

5. **(a)** In capitation, providers are responsible for a target population for which they receive an age- and gender-adjusted budget.

6. **(b)** "Certification is the formal recognition of the knowledge, skills, and experience demonstrated by the achievement of standards identified by the profession." (APRN Consensus Work Group, 2008, p. 6)

7. **(a)** "Case management is a collaborative process of assessment, planning, facilitation and advocacy for options and services to meet an individual's health needs through communication and available resources to promote quality cost- effective outcomes." (Case Management Society of America, 2003, p. 37)

8. **(d)** The NCQA certifies managed care plans utilizing a set of performance measures known as Health Plan Employer Data and Information Sets (HEDIS).

9. **(c)** The extent of prescription writing privileges varies from state to state.

10. **(a)** Clinical practice guidelines are systematically developed statements to assist practitioner and patient about appropriate care for specific clinical outcomes.

11. **(d)** Continuous quality improvement is considered to be an integral (not just periodic) part of the organization.

12. **(c)** Outcome measures reflect the effects of care on health status, patient knowledge, and satisfaction. Structural measures of care include the physical and organizational properties of the site, and process measures reflect what is actually done in giving and receiving care.

13. **(c)** Political activism through lobbying at local, state, and national levels is an example of coercive change strategies. The power of our vote will influence the actions of policy makers who represent us.

14. **(c)** EPSDT is intended to provide comprehensive care to Medicaid eligible individuals up to age 21.

15. **(d)** Scope of practice statements are prepared by national professional organizations and may go beyond what is legally allowable in a given state.

◘ REFERENCES

AACN. (2004). *AACN position statement on the practice doctorate in nursing.* Available at: http://www.aacn.nche.edu/DNP/DNP PositionStatement.htm. Accessed June 1, 2009.

APRN Consensus Work Group, & the National Council of State Boards of Nursing APRN Advisory Committee. (2008). Consensus model for APRN regulation: Licensure, accreditation, certification, & education. Available at: http://www.aacn.nche.edu/Education/pdf/APRNReport.pdf. Accessed April 24, 2009.

Byrne, W. (2009). US nurse practitioner prescribing law. A state-by-state summary. *Medscape Nurses.* Available at: http://www.medscape.com/viewarticle/440315. Accessed January 16, 2010.

Case Management Society of America. (2003 January-February). *The case report,* p. 37.

Christian, S., Dower, C., & O'Neill, E. O. (2004). *Chart overview of nurse practitioner scopes of practice in the United States.* San Francisco, CA: UCSF Center for the Health Professions.

CMS. (2003). *HIPAA 101 for health care providers' offices.* Available at: http://www.cms .hhs.gov/EducationMaterials/Downloads/ HIPAA101-1.pdf. Accessed June 1, 2009.

CMSA. (2008). *What is a case manager?* Available at: http://www.cmsa.org/Home/CMSA/ WhatisaCaseManager/tabid/224/Default .aspx. Accessed October 27, 2009.

Hansen-Turton, T., Ritter, A., & Torgan, R. (2008). Insurer's contracting policies on nurse practitioners as primary care providers. *Policy, Politics & Nursing Practice, 9,* 4, 241–248.

National Association of Pediatric Nurse Practitioners Staff. (2008). *Pediatric nursing: Scope and standards of practice.* Silver Spring, MD: American Nurses Publishing

NAPNAP. (2008). NAPNAP position on the Doctorate of Nursing Practice (DNP). *Journal of Pediatric Health Care, 22,* 4, 25A–26A. Available at: http://download .journals.elsevierhealth.com/pdfs/journals/ 0891-5245/PIIS0891524508001314.pdf. Accessed May 27, 2009.

National Task Force on Quality Nurse Practitioner Education. (2008). *Criteria for evaluation of nurse practitioner programs.* Washington, DC: National Organization of Nurse Practitioner Faculties.

NCSBN. (2010). *Licensure.* Available at: https:// www.ncsbn.org/256.htm. Accessed February 17, 2010

Nurse Practitioner Roundtable. (2008, June). *Nurse practitioner DNP education, certification and titling: A unified statement.* Washington, DC: Author.

Index

Univ of Maryland/Baltimore
222 North Pine Street
Baltimore, MD 21201
(410) 328-7788

Univ. of Maryland Baltimore

STORE:06390   REG:001   TRAN#:7210
CASHIER:JENNIFER S

WHITE CHEDDAR POPC
072600002258   T
(1 @ 0.99)   0.99
Pediatric Nurse Pr
TRADE
9780763776268   T
(1 @ 35.95) *   35.95
Seasonal
042823102295   T
(1 @ 2.29)   2.29

Subtotal   39.23
 T1 Sales Tax (06.000%)   2.35
TOTAL   41.58
MASTERCARD   41.58
  Card#: XXXXXXXXXXXXX9769
  Expdate: XX/XX
  Auth: 01562B
  Entry Method: Swiped

I AGREE TO PAY ABOVE TOTAL AMOUNT
ACCORDING TO CARD ISSUER AGREEMENT

Textbook sales are final

V240.50   09/15/2011 05:16PM

CUSTOMER COPY

- eBooks.
- Textbooks must be in original condition.
- No refunds or exchanges without original receipt.

GENERAL READING BOOKS, SOFTWARE, AUDIO, VIDEO & SMALL ELECTRONICS
- A full refund will be given in your original form of payment if merchandise is returned within 14 days of purchase with original receipt.
- Opened software, audio books, DVDs, CDs, music, and small electronics may not be returned. They can be exchanged for the same item if defective.
- Merchandise must be in original condition.
- No refunds or exchanges without original receipt.

ALL OTHER MERCHANDISE
- A full refund will be given in your original form of payment with original receipt.
- Without a receipt, a store credit will be issued at the current selling price.
- Cash back on merchandise credits or gift cards will not exceed $1.
- No refunds on gift cards, prepaid cards, phone cards, newspapers, or magazines.
- Merchandise must be in original condition.

Fair Pricing Policy
Barnes & Noble College Booksellers comply with local weights & measures requirements. If the price on your receipt is above the advertised or posted price, please alert a bookseller and we will gladly refund the difference.

REFUND POLICY

TEXTBOOKS:
- A full refund will be given in your original form of payment if textbooks are returned during the first week of classes with original receipt.
- With proof of a schedule change and original receipt, a full refund will be given in your original form of payment during the first 30 days of classes.
- No refunds on unwrapped loose leaf books or activated eBooks.
- Textbooks must be in original condition.
- No refunds or exchanges without original receipt.

GENERAL READING BOOKS, SOFTWARE, AUDIO, VIDEO & SMALL ELECTRONICS
- A full refund will be given in your original form of payment if merchandise is returned within 14 days of purchase with original receipt.
- Opened software, audio books, DVDs, CDs, music, and small electronics may not be returned. They can be exchanged for the same item if defective.
- Merchandise must be in original condition.
- No refunds or exchanges without original receipt.

ALL OTHER MERCHANDISE
- A full refund will be given in your original form of payment with original receipt.
- Without a receipt, a store credit will be issued at the current selling price.
- Cash back on merchandise credits or gift cards will not exceed $1.
- No refunds on gift cards, prepaid cards, phone cards